LEWIS L. GOULD

The Spanish-American War
and
PRESIDENT McKINLEY

UNIVERSITY PRESS OF KANSAS

Published by the University Press of Kansas (Lawrence, Kansas 66045),
which was organized by the Kansas Board of Regents and is operated and
funded by Emporia State University, Fort Hays State University, Kansas
State University, Pittsburg State University, the University of Kansas, and
Wichita State University

Library of Congress Cataloging in Publication Data

Gould, Lewis L.
The Spanish-American War and President McKinley.

"Based on an earlier study, The presidency of William
McKinley"—Pref.
Bibliography: p.
Includes index.
1. United States—History—War of 1898. 2. McKinley,
William, 1843–1901. I. Gould, Lewis L. The presidency
of William McKinley. II. Title.
E715.G66   1982   973.8'8'0924   82-13672
ISBN 0-7006-0227-5

Printed in the United States of America

Contents

List of Illustrations

Preface

This volume is based on an earlier study, *The Presidency of William McKinley* (Lawrence: Regents Press of Kansas, 1980). Since the Spanish-American War was the decisive event of McKinley's years in the White House, the three chapters on the coming of the conflict, the war itself, and the making of peace formed a natural unit. I have provided an opening chapter, which brings McKinley and his administration to the brink of the diplomatic controversy with Spain, and a concluding chapter, which traces the consequences that followed the ratification of the Peace of Paris. These two chapters also draw freely on material in the book on McKinley's presidency. By concentrating on McKinley and the war, I hope that students and colleagues will be able to examine why this conflict was a turning point in American foreign policy and the evolution of the modern presidency. This book thus attempts to fill the need for a brief, up-to-date analysis of how presidential policy under McKinley shaped American entry into the war, brought the fighting to a successful conclusion, and acquired an empire while achieving peace with Spain.

R. Hal Williams, Paul Holbo, and Herbert F. Margulies read and criticized the author's work in their usual cooperative and analytical spirit. Mrs. Bonnie Montgomery typed several drafts with customary good humor and exemplary efficiency. Karen Gould has provided loyal support and cheerful inspiration through several years of work on McKinley and his times.

Lewis L. Gould
Austin, Texas
April 1982

1

PRESIDENT McKINLEY

On March 3, 1897, Washington, D.C., was in readiness for the inauguration the next day of William McKinley as the twenty-fifth president. A close friend of the new chief executive, Charles G. Dawes, wrote in his diary: "The streets were crowded—the hotel is full to overflowing and an air of expectancy is abroad. The army of office-seekers has its advance guard here." That evening, President Grover Cleveland invited McKinley to dinner at the White House. They talked about Cuba and the dangers of war with Spain. Cleveland told friends that McKinley said: "Mr. President, if I can only go out of office, at the end of my term, with the knowledge that I have done what lay in my power to avert this terrible calamity, with the success that has crowned your patience and persistence, I shall be the happiest man in the world."[1]

Thirteen months later, on April 20, 1898, President McKinley signed a congressional resolution that authorized him to intervene at once to end the fighting in Cuba between Spain and those who were rebelling against its rule. The goal, the resolution added, was "a stable and independent government" for the people of the island. A senator who was present at the signing ceremony in McKinley's office said: "This is a historic occasion; you are virtually signing the declaration of War, Mr. President."[2] Within five days, Spain and the United States were at war. When the conflict ended three months later, Spain had been defeated, the Americans were in possession of Puerto Rico and Guam, and there were United States armies on the soil of Cuba and the Philippines.

1

McKinley had not been able to escape the war during his presidency, but his conduct of diplomacy leading up to the outbreak of hostilities, his leadership during the war, and his negotiation of peace combined to give his administration its significant place in the nation's history.

McKinley has never come into clear historical focus. Gray and dull beside the pinwheel ebullience of Theodore Roosevelt, he has remained a catchword for Republican conservatism or an inviting target for scholars who find his Victorian values either cloying or hypocritical. These attacks are badly off the mark. The wife of a political associate once wrote of "the masks he wore!"[3] McKinley built a public personality with great shrewdness; he admitted few men to the reality behind the façade. So deftly did the various aspects of his character blend together to form a politician of wide national appeal that critics and enemies who sought an explanation for McKinley's emergence looked at any force or circumstance but the candidate himself.

McKinley is responsible for a good part of the mystery. Never a discursive letter writer before he became president, he apparently made a conscious decision to restrict his personal correspondence while in office. From 1898 on, the pressure of work confirmed his course on this point; therefore the student of his administration lacks the rambling, dictated effusions that Theodore Roosevelt provided to his biographers. Reconstructing McKinley's thought processes is very difficult; it requires the accumulation of evidence from his earlier career, small clues, some inference, and a close knowledge of his working habits.

A Civil War veteran and a lawyer in northeastern Ohio, McKinley entered politics in the 1870s and was elected to Congress as a Republican in 1876. By 1890 he had attained power as chairman of the Ways and Means Committee; nevertheless he was defeated in the election that year over the tariff issue. He quickly recovered, winning the Ohio governorship in 1891 and again in 1893, retiring from that office as the front runner for the Republican presidential nomination in 1896. At the party's convention in St. Louis, he easily beat his divided and dispirited competitors.

During his campaign, which he conducted from his front porch in Canton, McKinley, who was fifty-three, attracted newspapermen. The British reporter George W. Steevens, who visited the candidate on October 1, 1896, found a "strong, clean-shaven face" with "clear eyes, wide nose, full lips—all his features suggest dominant will and energy rather than subtlety of mind or emotion." Only five feet six and sensitive about his height, McKinley, in well-tailored clothes and stern bearing, sought to seem taller than he actually was. He was addicted to cigars, though he was never photographed with one, and Steevens saw that he was also "not unmindful of the spitoon."[4] Despite Steevens's pleas, McKinley would not be interviewed, and the journalist had to content himself with the nominee's set speech to his visitors.

In 1896 the public McKinley could be summed up in a few ready phrases. He was the champion of the protective tariff, a cause he had advanced since entering Congress. Defeated in the 1890 election, when the Democrats exploited popular apprehension about higher prices as a result of the Republican tariff measure, McKinley said in a friend's newspaper: "Protection was never stronger than it is at this hour." The panic of 1893 made his linkage of the tariff with economic well-being both plausible and popular.[5] Ten years after proclaiming that he was a high protectionist, McKinley had added an important variation to his tariff philosophy. While he was working on the McKinley Tariff Act, he had become a convert to James G. Blaine's concept of reciprocity. Envisioning the controlled reductions of tariff rates through treaties with the nation's trading partners, reciprocity promised both to forestall more drastic revision of protected schedules and to expand American markets overseas.[6]

His popular standing as the spokesman for the Republicans' central economic doctrine was the core of McKinley's appeal, but other elements enhanced his position within the GOP. As congressman and governor, he had mastered the demanding political environment of Ohio in a way that made him the embodiment of Republicanism in its midwestern heartland. Though he saw the future of the nation as being linked with the health of business, he found no necessary disharmony between labor and management. From the time of an early case in which he defended striking miners and through the labor disputes during his governorship, he was even-handed in dealing with strikes, sympathetic to unions, and able to demonstrate to industrial laborers how the tariff worked to their benefit. On the touchy ethnic and religious questions that often shaped local politics, he was tolerant and inclusive. His personal experience with bankruptcy in 1893 did nothing to injure his popularity. If anything, his national reputation grew when Americans learned how a friend's business failure had involved McKinley because of notes that he had endorsed. Even the private funding that relieved him of his debts did not destroy the public's perception of him as being an unwitting victim of the general economic distress.

The country became familiar with McKinley in the 1880s and 1890s as he crossed the nation, speaking on behalf of Republican candidates and causes. He enjoyed traveling, and so he came naturally to the journeying that marked his presidency. In front of an audience, McKinley was an effective orator in an age that venerated that now vanished art. During his presidential race he still displayed his capacity even to make statistics about the tariff more than the stuff of an arid recitation. Once in the White House, his speeches, all of which he wrote, tended to be shorter, more abstract, and, to the modern ear, often less specific. His listeners supplied the context and grasped the message in ways that gave his utterances great influence.

When people spoke of McKinley in his prime, they used such words as "dignity," "kindness," and "understanding." The tragedies of his personal life—two daughters had died in infancy, and his wife was virtually an invalid—closed off his private life from the public, who saw him as an example of marital devotion and appropriate reserve. McKinley once said to Charles W. Fairbanks, "Never keep books in politics,"[7] and he avoided making unnecessary enemies through recriminations or vengeance. He possessed charm, tact, and an ability to put himself in the place of others. After his death the theme of his small acts of thoughtfulness ran through the memorials to him.

Because he had so many friends, McKinley faced the charge that he had no firm convictions and that he gained affection and popularity by being weak and compliant. Opponents pointed to his pragmatic course on the money issue, where he responded to inflationary pressures in Ohio and was never a staunch advocate of a rigid gold standard. Joseph G. Cannon, in a notorious gibe, said that McKinley's ear was so close to the ground it was full of grasshoppers.

Buttressing the apparent impression that McKinley was the instrument of the will of others was his friendship with the Cleveland industrialist Marcus A. Hanna. The two men met first in the 1870s but did not become a political team until the period between 1888 and 1892. Hanna, who was fifty-nine in 1896, had been a force in Ohio politics for more than a decade. The relationship was easily caricatured in contemporary cartoons, and the notion lingers that Hanna made McKinley president when, in fact, the politician used the businessman to reach the White House. Mc-

Kinley needed the organizational skills and fund-raising ability that Hanna brought to politics. Their intimacy was always a political rather than a personal one, however; there were lines regarding behavior that Hanna knew he must never cross. Their friendship, which was at its height in 1896, would undergo important alterations once the new president had been inaugurated.

McKinley's ascendancy in his dealings with Hanna was characteristic of his management of people generally. "He had a way of handling men," said Elihu Root, "so that they thought his ideas were their own." Listening more than he talked, even being patient with those who bored him, McKinley moved toward his objectives steadily and unobtrusively. "He was a man of great power," Root continued, "because he was absolutely indifferent to credit. His great desire was 'to get it done.' He cared nothing about the credit, but McKinley *always had his way*."[8] From such men as Elihu Root, William Howard Taft, and John Hay, the president secured exemplary service and enduring respect.

Whether they were his critics who assailed him or his friends who idolized him, most men who knew McKinley recognized that he kept the core of his personality away from public view. The private McKinley had a strain of stoicism and reserve that made him a cold and, on occasion, a ruthless figure. He possessed ambition and a sense of his own destiny, traits that he usually kept well hidden. "I don't think that McKinley every let anything stand in the way of his own advancement," said Senator Charles Dick in 1906. "McKinley was not altogether to blame for this trait in his character. He had been petted and flattered until he felt that all the fruit on the tree was his."[9] Dick knew that McKinley always gave a little less than he received from friends. The Major could use and discard people when it suited his purposes.

As a political leader, McKinley had the defects of his qualities. Charisma was not a concept that McKinley would have understood. If he pleased Americans, whose goodness he affirmed, he did not frequently inspire them. He surrounded the presidency with a dignity that became almost imperial by 1900, but there was never the drama that Theodore Roosevelt or Woodrow Wilson supplied. The party, the Congress, and the nation moved toward the president's goals in small, cumulative steps without a sense of passing from one great event to another. When McKinley died, his political approach disappeared, leaving large results but few traces of their architect.

It was easy to find weaknesses in McKinley's style of governance. The president's adversaries usually lost, but after innumerable minor wounds rather than one decisive stroke. While he triumphed by a process of attrition, his patience seemed to be evasion, his maneuvering to be irresolution, and his compromises to be defeat. Sometimes these harsh judgments were true; usually they were not. In fact, he was an important contributor to the emergence of the modern presidency.

After an exciting election campaign in 1896, which aroused significant popular interest, McKinley won a decisive victory over the nominee of the Democrats and the Populists, William Jennings Bryan. In 1894 the nation had shifted toward the Republicans in the congressional elections. McKinley's margin of nearly six hundred thousand votes was the largest in a quarter of a century, and a long period of Republican ascendancy had opened. The GOP had assembled a winning coalition of urban residents in the North, prosperous farmers, industrial workers, and most ethnic groups except the Irish. Though electoral trends now favored the Republicans, the unhappy experience of Grover Cleveland's administration indicated that changing circumstances and poor leadership could produce sudden realignments. It became the political task of the new president to bring the prosperity that he had promised and to see that the Republican victory was not transitory.

Between the election of 1896 and his inauguration in March 1897, McKinley spent most of his time assembling his cabinet. Three appointments would have a direct impact on the impending crisis over Cuba. The first was simple. John Davis Long of Massachusetts and the incoming president had been colleagues in the House during the 1880s, and Long was popular in New England, an area that was responsive to the flow of naval appropriations. On January 30, 1897, McKinley offered Long the post as secretary of the navy. Although McKinley had reservations about Theodore Roosevelt's temperament, he accepted the urgings of Senator Henry Cabot Lodge of Massachusetts and others to name the young New Yorker as assistant secretary of the navy. Having been assured that the candidate had "no preconceived plans which he would wish to drive through the moment he got in,"[10] the president appointed the popular and charismatic Roosevelt in April 1897.

The secretary of war was not a job that in 1896 evoked images of guns firing and armies marching. The peacetime army, with twenty-five thousand officers and men, had only a modest military role. Politicians looked upon it as an agency whose civilian responsibilities—exploration, flood relief, and construction on rivers and harbors—required business experience in order to be properly managed. Given such assumptions, the candidacy of Russell A. Alger of Michigan made sense to McKinley. At sixty-one, Alger had a record of military service in the Civil War, which had brought him the rank of general, success in the lumber industry in Michigan, and a career in politics as governor and favorite-son presidential candidate in 1888.

Before naming Alger in late January, McKinley checked into the substance of the aspirant's war record to refute charges that he had resigned from the army in 1864 under a cloud. Having established Alger's fitness to serve in the last war, the president-elect did not take up the issue of how his choice might handle a future conflict. Alger's business and governmental record was less impressive than it appeared. Neither as an industrial executive nor as governor of Michigan had he displayed the capacity to meet the larger responsibilities of war. Alger was not an utter disaster as secretary of war, but he was over his head when the Spanish-American War came. At the time of his designation, the *Brooklyn Eagle* noted: "We certainly tremble to contemplate the outcome of a war conducted under his direction."[11] McKinley erred in not giving careful thought to that eventuality, and his administration suffered as a result.

The choice of John Sherman as secretary of state became the most controversial of McKinley's cabinet appointments because of Sherman's failure in the post and because Mark Hanna succeeded him in the United States Senate. Had McKinley picked Sherman, heedless of Sherman's waning mental powers, in order to provide Hanna with a place in Congress? It is clear that Hanna wanted to be a senator and that he saw the opportunity, if Sherman were to go into the new administration, to achieve a goal that he had quietly desired for some years. McKinley would have preferred to have Hanna in the cabinet as a clearly defined subordinate, and he offered his friend the postmaster generalship in mid November. Hanna refused, proposing instead to sound out Sherman about becoming secretary of state. McKinley agreed to let the subject be explored, and newspapers reported Hanna's ideas by the last week in November.

John Sherman, at seventy-three, was approaching the end of the Senate term that he had won in 1892. He now faced the prospect of retiring in 1899, waging a hard race for reelection to the Senate, or finishing his public life with a cabinet post. Having been secretary of the treasury under Rutherford B. Hayes, he could only gain further fame in the State Department. Hanna and Sherman had once been political allies, and on November 13, 1896, the senator wrote to his former associate: "If you wish to enter political life, I would like to be one of your backers." When word of Hanna's scheme circulated, Sherman dismissed the reports. In early December, however, the two men met and discussed the subject. On December 15 Sherman told Hanna that he had made up his mind to say yes if McKinley offered him the State Department portfolio.[12]

If McKinley were part of a plot by Hanna to elevate Sherman so as to create a senatorial opening, McKinley's next actions were hardly designed to complete the transaction. With Sherman's agreement in hand, the president-elect authorized his emissaries in Iowa to approach Senator William Boyd Allison about the State Department post. In the week before Christmas, Allison indicated that he was not interested and would not accept the position if it were offered to him. Informed of these facts shortly after the holiday, McKinley now viewed Sherman as an attractive option. On January 4, 1897, he wrote the senator: "I would very much like to have you in my administration as Sec'y of State." The letter was delivered on January 6, and McKinley's agent reported: "I could see that he was delighted to receive it."[13]

After leaving the cabinet in 1898, Sherman wrote that McKinley and Hanna had "deprived me of the high office of Senator by the temporary appointment as Secretary of State."[14] By then, Sherman had forgotten that he had taken the cabinet appointment voluntarily, indeed with some eagerness. Anxious about his reelection, Sherman was quite willing to occupy the place for his own advantage. As to whether it was to be a "temporary" term of office, McKinley expected the future secretary to serve for at least two years. Sherman's tenure was shorter because of his own incapacity, not as a result of any prearrangement by McKinley.

Would Sherman have been a candidate if Hanna had not had any ambitions for the Senate? Among Republican elders, Sherman stood on the same level of popular reputation as Allison, and he ranked higher than Nelson Aldrich of Rhode Island or Orville H. Platt of Connecticut. Sherman could hardly have been ignored in the cabinet-making process. The central question is whether McKinley knew that Sherman lacked the physical and mental resources that the job required. That Sherman's intelligence had faded somewhat was well known in Washington. McKinley was aware of some of this talk, but he had heard from a close friend in December that Sherman's mind was very clear. After the appointment had been announced, when talk of the prospective secretary's deficiencies was widespread, the new president wrote angrily: "When I saw him last I was convinced both of his perfect health, physically and mentally, and that his prospects of life were remarkably good."[15]

Despite these claims, McKinley had not checked thoroughly enough into Sherman's condition, nor had Sherman's family hastened to enlighten the president-elect about the senator's health. Expecting to be his own secretary of state and intending to have his friend William R. Day as Sherman's first assistant in due course, McKinley had made an expedient choice. The extent of the misjudgment emerged quickly. Sherman was one of the few advisors who was invited to offer suggestions for the inaugural address. He responded with a draft on the Cuban problem that threatened American intervention in the island. The memorandum silently disappeared, but the Sherman problem lingered on. Hanna achieved his goal of the Senate in late February, which added to the impression that Sherman was secretary of state because of a deal with McKinley and Hanna.

How the new president would handle foreign policy remained one of the puzzles of the transitional period. Since his political career had focused on internal politics during an era when international problems were only sporadically an issue, he entered upon the presidency without a well-defined record in that field. When Grover Cleveland's annual message in December 1895 challenged Great Britain on the Monroe Doctrine over Venezuela, McKinley told reporters that what the president had done "enforces with strength and vigor the position of the United States in its relations with European powers for more than seventy years. It is American in letter and spirit, and its calm and dispassionate manner upholds the honor of the Nation and insures its security." He said little on the Cuban problem in 1895 and 1896. A writer on foreign policy in April 1897 remarked about McKinley: "We know more about him than during the last forty years we have known of any other President up to the hour of his taking office." Nevertheless, politicians interested in diplomatic questions did not display a confidence about where McKinley stood. Henry Cabot Lodge visited him in Canton in December 1896, asked him about Hawaii, Cuba, and other matters, and then told Theodore Roosevelt, with a trace of surprise, "his whole attitude of mind struck me as serious, broad in view, and just what we all ought to desire."[16]

The apparent vagueness of McKinley's public utterances before entering the White House does not indicate the full extent of his preparation for conducting foreign policy. His favorite subject, the tariff, while seemingly a domestic question, required a grasp of international commerce, and McKinley's wide reading in the statistics of world trade is evident from the speeches of his protectionist phase. As he shifted his emphasis to reciprocity after 1891, his outlook correspondingly broadened still more.

Throughout his presidency, men seemed to be surprised when McKinley showed himself to be well informed on international bimetallism, the annexation of Hawaii, the tariff laws of the nation's trading partners, or the currents of world politics generally. They should not have been. As a congressman he understood the significance of Pearl Harbor to American interests in Hawaii. He argued for an improved and revitalized merchant marine, and he encouraged naval expansion while he was in office. He told Robert M. La Follette that he hoped "to round out his career by gaining for America a supremacy in the markets of the world . . . without weakening the protective system." By the end of his presidency, foreign observers were calling him "a man of will and perseverance" who wished to break down the foreign tariffs that were excluding American exports.[17]

Shortly after becoming president, McKinley informed Carl Schurz: "You may be sure there will be no jingo nonsense under my administration."[18] Schurz naturally took this comment as a pledge against expansion, but McKinley probably meant that his foreign policy would pursue economic and political expansion in a decorous and methodical way. The Republican platform of 1896, which reflected McKinley's ideas, sought a Nicaraguan canal, American control of Hawaii, and purchase of the Danish West Indies. In office, McKinley moved promptly to achieve the annexation of Hawaii, to secure American rights to an isthmian canal, and to broaden the nation's foreign commerce. As an advocate of penetrating the overseas markets, William McKinley was aware of those in the United States who thought that a surplus of manufactured products would threaten social stability. Overproduction, if not resolved through expanded markets, could, in his view, both perpetuate the economic distress of the depression and threaten drastic change in the political order.

For his part, McKinley conceived of the spread of American trade as a positive, benevolent force. Convinced of the soundness of the nation's institutions and believing that citizens of the United States achieved morally defensible goals when they extended capitalism outside America's borders, he thought that measures to enhance his country's economic influence were in the nation's best interest.

The diffusion of United States commerce did not, in practice, prove to be as simple and beneficent as it was depicted to be in articles and campaign speeches. Experience in the Caribbean and in Asia revealed to men like McKinley the complexities of such an apparently straightforward goal as "the extension of trade to be followed by wider markets, better fields of employment, and easier conditions for the masses."[19] Some later historians, reflecting on the record of American imperialism after 1898, came to regard the language of McKinley and his generation as fatuous and hypocritical. Who could believe any longer that the pursuit of the national interest of the United States could be a positive good? McKinley did; and the shape of his foreign policy evolved from the premise that greater power and influence for his nation would also promote the betterment of mankind.

The new administration launched a number of diplomatic initiatives during its first year. In the areas of trade and finance, McKinley opened negotiations with France and Great Britain toward an international bimetallic agreement to promote greater use of silver in the world. The idea was to stabilize silver prices and to defuse free-silver sentiment in the United States. The talks failed when in the late summer the British, the champions of the gold standard, rejected a Franco-American bimetallic proposal. After the protectionist Dingley Tariff became law in July, the State Department began talks with France and other countries about tariff-reciprocity agreements and treaties that the new tariff legislation authorized.[20]

Relations with Great Britain also received presidential attention. In the wake of the Venezuelan crisis of 1895, Grover Cleveland's secretary of state, Richard Olney, had concluded a general arbitration treaty with the British in January 1897. In his inaugural address, McKinley, who had been a proponent of labor arbitration in railroad disputes during the 1880s, cited the precedents and process that had led up to the Olney-Pauncefote Treaty, and he gave it his support. Despite this presidential push, the treaty, much amended, failed in the Senate on May 5, 1897.[21]

Other efforts to improve Anglo-American affairs brought more results. Eager to establish an ascendancy in the Caribbean, the United States wanted to remove the obstacle that the Clayton-Bulwer Treaty of 1850 posed with regard to an American canal in

Central America. To achieve that purpose required resolution of disputes over such disparate questions as fur seals in the Bering Sea, fisheries in Newfoundland, and, most sensitive of all, the Alaskan boundary with Canada. The Alaskan problem grew in importance with the discovery of gold in the Yukon and the resulting flow of population into the disputed area. Early in 1898, American negotiators proposed the establishment of a joint high commission of Canadian and United States representatives. Several months later, in an interview with the British ambassador, McKinley suggested that the commission be promptly created and that all outstanding issues be left to its deliberations. By August 1898 the work of the commission had begun. Many difficulties remained ahead in Anglo-American relations, but the essential direction of McKinley's policy had been established. The start of the rapprochement with Great Britain would be a positive aspect for American policy makers when the war with Spain began.[22]

The persistent question of the annexation of Hawaii became a significant component of McKinley's diplomatic activity in the Pacific. Throughout his first year the president pushed hard for United States acquisition of the islands in a manner that foreshadowed future uses of his executive leadership. Republican support for annexation of Hawaii had been longstanding. After a revolution in Hawaii in 1893, the lame-duck Harrison administration sent the Senate a treaty of annexation. Grover Cleveland, who disapproved of American involvement in the revolt, probed its circumstances and withdrew the pact. In 1896 the Republican platform asserted that the United States should control the islands and prevent foreign interference. The friends of annexation, both on the islands and among American expansionists, looked expectantly to McKinley for positive action. Before he was inaugurated, he was characteristically reticent. "Of course I have my ideas about Hawaii," he told representatives from Hawaii in November 1896, "but consider that it is best at the present time not to make known what my policy is."[23]

Once in office, McKinley pursued a course that revealed his determination to add Hawaii to the territory of the United States. On March 12 he discussed with John W. Foster (Harrison's secretary of state) and Senator William P. Frye of Maine the merits of pursuing annexation either by treaty or by joint congressional resolution. Two weeks later, McKinley informed another visiting Hawaiian delegation that once the tariff problem had been resolved, annexation would receive his early attention. On April 3 Hawaii's minister officially asked the United States to open talks about a treaty. With the debate over the tariff going on in Congress, with office seekers besieging the White House, and with Secretary Sherman's liabilities as a cabinet officer becoming apparent, the administration indicated that early action on Hawaii was not likely.[24]

The president and his cabinet were, however, particularly sensitive to the problem of growing Japanese immigration into the islands. Because of the influx of laborers from Japan, the Hawaiian government had refused in March to admit the latest contingent of immigrants. The Japanese sent one of their naval vessels to Hawaii in May, and their minister gave out strident interviews that suggested the possibility of more drastic action. The American navy, which drafted a war plan against Japan in the spring, expanded its force of vessels in the islands. In May the administration asked Foster to prepare a draft annexation treaty, which was transmitted to the president at the end of the month.[25]

By early June, McKinley decided to send the treaty to Congress. Because dispatches from Hawaii were warning of Japanese pressure, the administration instructed the American naval commander on June 10 that, if the Japanese used force, he should "land a suitable force, and announce officially provisional assumption of protectorate pending ratification of treaty of annexation." In Congress the Republican senatorial caucus also seemed to be ready to discard the reciprocity treaty of 1875 and to bar Hawaiian sugar from the American market. Foreign and domestic influences converged as the president revised Foster's draft treaty, the Hawaiian representatives were summoned on June 11, and the signing ceremony was set for June 16 when Secretary Sherman would be back in Washington. After a cabinet meeting, the treaty was signed, and a message was sent to Congress. Annexation, McKinley wrote, "despite successive denials and postponements, has been merely a question of time." It was "not a change. It is a consummation."[26]

There was no hope that the Senate would act on the treaty at the special session of Congress, for it was preoccupied by preparation of the Dingley Tariff law. Meanwhile, the Japanese protested that "the maintenance of the status quo of Hawaii is essential to the good understanding of the Powers that have interests in the Pacific." The administration took additional naval precautions against possible Japanese action during the summer of 1897, and officials such as Theodore Roosevelt remarked publicly that the nation did not have to ask other powers about acquiring territory. McKinley told Senator George Frisbie Hoar of Massachusetts: "If something be not done, there will be before long another Revolution, and Japan will get control." The immediate problem ebbed away in diplomatic correspondence, and the Japanese eventually withdrew their protest in December 1897.[27]

When Congress reconvened in December, McKinley's problem was to find a two-thirds majority for the treaty. Three Republicans opposed annexation, but the bulk of the opposition came from the Democrats, especially southerners, who disliked the racial mix of Hawaii's people. Beet-sugar interests, fearful of Hawaiian sugar, also worked against the pact. McKinley wanted the treaty to be acted on promptly. He worked on senators on behalf of approval, and Henry Cabot Lodge decided in early January 1898 that "annexation has been gaining steadily since Congress met, and we are near now the necessary two thirds." Lodge was too optimistic. The annexation forces were two or three votes short of two-thirds as January began, and despite McKinley's exertions, the balance remained stable throughout February and into March. By the middle of March, advocates of the treaty conceded that they could not obtain a two-thirds majority. With the Cuban crisis impending, it was decided to shift to a joint resolution, which required only a simple majority, once pending legislation and troubles with Spain had been resolved.[28]

The Hawaiian campaign disclosed McKinley's willingness to exercise presidential power on behalf of his legislative program. So persistent was he that opposition such as the *Nation* wondered why he was "so busy and earnest" about Hawaii. The president, reported Sanford B. Dole, president of the islands, "seems to have heart and soul in the annexation treaty." McKinley's comment to his secretary, George B. Cortelyou, revealed his priorities in June 1898: "We need Hawaii just as much and a good deal more than we did California. It is manifest destiny." Once the Cuban crisis had been faced, the president would return to the Hawaiian issue and renew a campaign that represented one of his early attempts to woo Congress on behalf of his foreign-policy objectives.[29]

By the end of 1897 McKinley had taken the direction of diplomacy into his own hands. Secretary Sherman showed his decreasing mental capacity in several unfortunate interviews on sensitive topics. Deaf and forgetful, the secretary became an embarrassment to the administration, and the running of his department passed to William R. Day. Clearly, Sherman would have to go, but it was not easy to find the right time, given the difficulties with Spain.

In his first year in the White House, McKinley had done much to revive presidential power from the blows it had received during the second Cleveland administration. He was more open and accessible than his predecessor had been. The sentry boxes and detectives that had surrounded the residence vanished, and visitors were welcomed rather than discouraged. "The feeling that the executive mansion was a place, exclusive, reserved, and guarded has disappeared." McKinley also traveled more than Cleveland had done, and his readiness to use the mobility of his office would be an important asset once the war with Spain was over.[30]

Relations with the press, to which the president devoted quiet attention, also flourished. A long table was set up on the second floor, where reporters assigned to the White House had seats. The president's secretary, John Addison Porter, circulated constantly, and at noon and 4:00 P.M. he spoke formally with the newsmen. A system of releases for presidential messages and important announcements was created, and the White House looked to the interests of the press corps. The president did not give interviews and was not to be quoted directly, but reporters had greater access to him as president than students of his press relations have realized. McKinley's deft handling of the journalists in his first year not only reestablished the White House as a significant source of news; it also was a large step in the enhancing of presidential power.[31]

The chief executive worked in the president's offices, on the second floor of the White House. Using the Cabinet Room as his private office in order to escape those who waited to see him, he sat at the head of a long table in a swivel armchair with ink, stationery, and books at hand. Beneath a portrait of Thomas Jefferson and in front of a crowded bookcase, McKinley, in long coat, high collar, and bow tie, scratched out the handwriting that could, on an Executive Mansion card, obtain an appointment with a cabinet officer or gain a hearing for a job applicant. Though he deliberately wrote few personal letters, McKinley wanted all mail to be acknowledged, and he wanted letters to be directed to the appropriate department. Presidential letters did go out to veterans' organizations, labor unions, and charitable or religious bodies for their annual conventions or special occasions. A never-ending pile of clippings, letters, and memoranda passed before a hard-working executive, who labored into the evening in the comfortable surroundings he had created.

Success for McKinley's executive style depended on the quality of his personal secretary. The president specified that the formal title should be secretary to the president, and he hoped that John

Addison Porter would be the useful aide on whom he must rely. Porter, who had been an early supporter in Connecticut, was pompous and erratic. Soon he lost real power to George B. Cortelyou, a holdover from the Cleveland administration, who exercised impressive good sense and efficiency. Whether it involved arranging the tours that McKinley loved, working with the press, or acting as a presidential confidant, Cortelyou soon emerged as a prototype to the modern White House staff member.

McKinley and his cabinet met every Tuesday and Friday morning at eleven in the rundown and slightly shabby Cabinet Room. In their recollections, cabinet members have said that the president usually began with a brief anecdote and then turned to business. "Sometimes he led discussion," said Charles Emory Smith; "quite as often he first elicited the views of his counselors." Whatever their experience with McKinley, the cabinet officers knew who ran the administration. When John Sherman resigned, he wrote that McKinley "evinced a disposition to assume all the functions of the members of his Cabinet and especially of the duties of the State Department." On leaving office, Sherman added that McKinley's "cabinet counsels were not a free exchange of opinions but rather the mandates of a paramount ruler." Publicly, the president had nothing but praise for his cabinet. Nonetheless, Cortelyou, whose opinions followed those of McKinley, wrote at the height of the Cuban crisis: "It is a good working Cabinet but in some respects not a strong one, not strong in the direction of being trustworthy advisors of the President in great emergencies."[32]

On March 3, 1898, the Republican Club of the 28th Assembly District in New York gave a "Grand Ball . . . in commemoration of the first year of Republican National supremacy." At the end of McKinley's first twelve months, other evaluations, from less friendly sources, appeared. "With every desire to be fair," said the *New York World*, "it must be admitted that his Administration this far has been mediocre and unsatisfying."[33] Between these partisan assessments lay a measured record of accomplishments and failures. The Dingley Tariff had been passed in July 1897 without the congressional disruptions that had wounded Benjamin Harrison and Grover Cleveland; negotiations on tariff reciprocity had opened; and the administration had pursued international bimetallism until British opposition had killed the initiative. On domestic issues, McKinley was moving toward an affirmation of the gold standard in early 1898, and he had allocated the patronage among Republicans while preserving reasonable amity.

In the off-year elections the GOP had suffered the reverses that a party in power expected. Republican candidates lost in Nebraska, New Jersey, New York, and Kansas; the party vote fell off in Ohio and Pennsylvania. How the party would fare in the 1898 congressional races remained an open question. "While the Republicans do not concede that the Democrats are going to win, they admit that the result may be close," wrote a friendly reporter in February 1898. "At the best they hope for only a small majority in the next house."[34]

The outlines of McKinley's presidential style had also emerged during this year of executive apprenticeship. Improved relations with the press demonstrated that he understood how modern methods of communication could serve as a weapon of governmental leadership. Extensive travel had personalized the presidency and familiarized the electorate with the man in the White House. Six months into his term, McKinley had attained a level of personal popularity that gave him a powerful lever in public controversies. Wooing Congress on one level, McKinley had set in motion forces that would give him an ascendancy over the legislative branch as his term progressed. Within the executive branch he had tested subordinates. Some, such as Secretary of State Sherman, were quietly superseded, and others were marked for lesser jobs or eventual replacement. Though he lacked the bureaucratizing impulse of Theodore Roosevelt and a younger generation, McKinley emphasized formal procedures in the conduct of domestic and foreign policy that enhanced the role and power of the federal government. Imperceptibly but inexorably, the power of the presidency expanded under McKinley's deft direction. He left no overt statement that he intended to restore the prestige and authority to his office, but his actions during the first year reveal a president with an instinct for power and a clear purpose of augmenting it.

McKinley would need all the assets he had painstakingly amassed in 1897. Behind the varied diplomatic activity of the new administration lay the recurrent issue of Cuba and its effect on the nation's relations with Spain. The president had touched on the problem first in his inaugural address on March 4, 1897. When he praised George Washington's policy of "non-interference with the affairs of foreign governments," he added that the United States had been "content to leave undisturbed" with friends and enemies "the settlement of their own domestic concerns." Since Spain believed that the uprising in Cuba was an internal matter, the latter clause was mildly encouraging. Almost at once, however, the speech proposed "a firm and dignified foreign policy" that would insist upon "the enforcement of the lawful rights of American citizens everywhere."[35] What this meant for United States citizens and their property in Cuba was not revealed.

After rejecting Secretary of State Sherman's maladroit paragraphs on Cuba, McKinley had considered a noncommittal remark about holding off on a statement of his views. He also drafted a passage in which he expressed his sympathy for the Cuban people, noted that the nation had recognized the belligerency of earlier revolts against Spanish rule, and then concluded that a policy of nonintervention was best at that time. "We want no wars of conquest; we must avoid the temptation of territorial aggression," he said. "War should never be entered upon until every agency of peace has failed; peace is preferable to war in almost every contingency."[36]

Throughout 1897 the public, distracted with other concerns, was unaware of the downward spiral of Spanish-American relations. Inside the government, the Cuban question continued to be a source of worry. "There can be no doubt that the Administration feels extremely anxious on this point," wrote a friend of McKinley's in September 1897, "and in fact sees hardly any escape from a war within a comparatively short time."[37] As the McKinley administration entered its second year in March 1898, the prospects for a war with Spain were increasing daily. Despite elaborate diplomatic maneuvers from the time of the inauguration onward, the gap between the two nations was unbridgeable. McKinley stood on the edge of a conflict that would give his presidency its special character and would fix his historical reputation.

commenced hostilities indicates that his presidential leadership during the coming of war was more courageous and principled than his critics have realized.

General agreement exists about the conditions in Spain, Cuba, and the United States that created a context for conflict. On February 24, 1895, Cuban insurgents started a revolt against Spanish rule. The roots of the uprising went back to the unsuccessful rebellion of 1868 to 1878, a war that had stopped but whose underlying causes persisted. To long-term unhappiness with the arbitrary, inept, and corrupt supremacy of Spain was added economic distress in 1894. Duties imposed on Cuban sugar by the Wilson-Gorman Tariff crippled the island's principal industry. Leaders of the independence movement, which had been active since the early 1890s, decided in late 1894: "We must force the situation—precipitate the events." Though not all the elements of their plans were in place, fighting broke out in late February 1895.[1]

To win the war the Cubans followed a strategy that made the most of their limited military resources. Avoiding battles with the numerically superior Spanish, they directed their energy against the Cuban economy. By destroying crops, disrupting transportation, and engaging in incessant hit-and-run assaults, the rebels pinned down Spanish soldiers and ate away at the island's economy. The war aim of the revolutionaries remained clear and explicit throughout the two years before McKinley became president. In June 1896 Antonio Maceo said that when Cuba became free, it could "laugh at the negotiations which do not favor its independence." A year later a rebel leader in the United States, Tomas Estrada Palma, wrote: "The Cubans are more determined today than ever to accept nothing short of independence." To offers of autonomy under some form of Spanish rule and to all peace feelers from Madrid, the Cubans were equally opposed. If the rebels participated in the diplomatic process, they would insist on nothing less than independence.[2]

While thirty thousand soldiers fought for the rebellion inside Cuba, a junta in the United States raised money, sought to send weapons to the insurgents, and waged an effective propaganda war to win over American public opinion. The filibustering expeditions that the junta mounted required a naval response in order to maintain the provisions of American neutrality. The junta's access to the press and its ready supply of atrocity stories and eyewitness accounts of Spanish brutalities did much to sustain popular interest in Cuban affairs. The presence of the junta convinced the Spanish that the Americans were not doing all that they could to remain neutral,

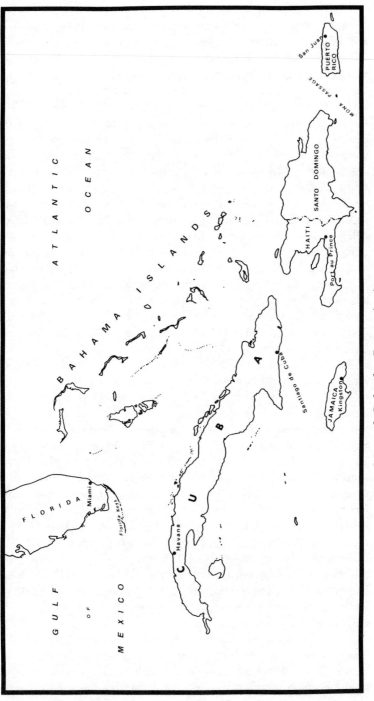

Map of Cuba by Lewis A. Armstrong

but the Cuban spokesmen had achieved such strong ties with labor, politicians, and Americans generally that their position was secure.

For Spain the outbreak of fighting in the "Ever Faithful Isle" admitted of only one possible response in 1895. The rebellion must be suppressed, and Spanish sovereignty must be preserved. In pursuit of that end the Madrid government committed several hundred thousand soldiers, who endured staggering casualties. Spanish deaths reached fifty thousand, and an equal number of men were wounded or became sick. Two successive commanders sought to defeat the rebellion. General Arsenio Martinez de Campos attempted, during the first year of the war, to repeat the success that he had achieved in 1878. By confining the revolt to the eastern part of Cuba, he hoped to use his superior numbers to destroy the guerillas. When this strategy failed to overcome the rebels, Spain replaced Campos with General Valeriano Weyler y Nicolau in January 1896. Appointed as a commander who would use repressive measures and proceed "with the greatest energy, without hesitations of any sort," Weyler adopted a "reconcentration" policy that was designed to destroy the popular base of the uprising. The Cuban people were moved out of the countryside and into fortified areas. Unsanitary conditions, overcrowding, and disease caused thousands of deaths, confirming the accuracy of Weyler's nickname, "Butcher," and still the rebellion went on.[3]

The war in Cuba placed great strain upon the fragile political structure of the Spanish nation. The human and economic cost aroused bitterness and discontent across the Iberian peninsula. One Spanish politician recalled a popular song of the day: "Today you are going to Cuba / You are going to Cuba / And you will never return." For the two major political parties, the Liberals and the Conservatives; for the shaky monarchy of the queen regent, Maria Cristina; and for the powerful armed forces, disputes over the way in which the war should be prosecuted did not shake a pervasive consensus about Cuba. The island was part of Spain, and Spanish sovereignty was not negotiable. "It is not possible," said the Spanish minister in Washington, Enrique Dupuy de Lôme, "to think that the Island of Cuba can be benefited except through the agency of Spain." Even war with the United States would be preferable to a negotiated humiliation.[4]

To a large extent, Spanish diplomacy toward the United States rested on the view that the passage of time would make the situation better. Perhaps the Cubans would yield; perhaps the Americans might become more sympathetic and restrain the rebels; perhaps other European powers would curb the United States. Meanwhile, the internal condition of Spanish society was too delicate and the sentiment for retaining Cuba was too strong to allow for more than token concessions over the issue. The Spanish held a weak hand, and procrastination and dissimulation accorded with what policy makers deemed to be the national interest. Diplomats and politicians never concealed their belief that a negotiated Cuban independence was intolerable, but they did not, understandably, point out that Americans erred when they believed that Spain would ultimately recognize that Cuba must be free. If Washington stated that Spain must relinquish Cuba, the two nations would hold mutually contradictory positions. Short of surrender, then, war would become inescapable.

Numerous forces, interwoven and reinforcing, animated American interest in the course of the Cuban revolt. Many citizens believed that Cubans should not suffer from the rule of Spain, a vestigial survivor of Europe in the New World. Periodic revolts tried the patience of the United States and strengthened the conviction that Spain had forfeited both its hold on Cuba and its place in the Western Hemisphere. Problems connected with preventing filibusterers from operating from American waters and with the fate of citizens who were caught up in the fighting were specific diplomatic irritants that arose out of this climactic rebellion.

Humanitarian and economic motives fused with historical experience over Cuba to shape popular attitudes. Accounts of atrocities resulting from the Spanish treatment of individuals were occasionally fabricated; more often they were verifiable. The horrors of the reconcentration policy were abundantly documented. Americans responded with funds for relief of the suffering, sympathy for the rebel cause, and pressure on the government to stop the fighting. Just because they were interested in the Cuban conflict did not mean that Americans had a well-defined perception of what should exist there after Spain had departed. In varying proportions, opinions favored the annexation of Cuba, diplomatic recognition of the rebels, or American military intervention. But the conviction grew, as the months of fighting passed, that something must be done.

The role of sensational journalism in creating an anti-Spanish mood in the United States has been one of the most scrutinized aspects of this subject. Did reporters furnish the ammunition, and did yellow-press publishers such as William Randolph Hearst of the *New York Journal* and Joseph Pulitzer of the *New York World* furnish a war? To newspapers that thrived on large headlines and

lurid reporting, Cuba was a natural running story, but it is too simple to assign primary blame for the conflict to Hearst and Pulitzer.
They printed colorful, exciting bulletins, some of which were true,
and they did not cool popular emotions. They served the propa-
gandistic purposes of the junta well, but they did not create the real
differences between the United States and Spain. They spoke for
only a small part of the journalistic community, and they reflected
what the public wanted, rather than shaping it.

The impact that the fighting had on the economic intimacy of
the United States and Cuba added tangible, realistic causes to the
former's concern over the island's future. Cuban-American trade,
which had already weakened during the depression, sagged; and the
destruction affected the $50 million that Americans had invested in
Cuba. More important in the minds of many businessmen, the persistence of uncertainty in relations with Spain—the possibility of
war—threatened to thwart recovery from the depression. Some in
the business community who had interests in Cuba favored intervention; the rest, including many investors in the island and a substantial body of opinion on Wall Street, wanted war to be avoided
and the economic suspense to be relieved. The extent of business
influence on McKinley's foreign policy has been overrated, but no
administration could ignore what the continuation of property
depredations, violence, and chaos in Cuba could mean to the
American economy.

Beyond the emotions that events in Cuba stirred lay the im-
measurable effect of general expansionist sentiment within the
United States in the 1890s. Historians still debate how the elements
of imperialism interacted to make the nation a world power, but
they agree on some causes that a plausible explanation must include.
A search for overseas markets to counter alleged industrial overproduction moved some low-tariff publicists and businessmen to
advocate not only the expansion of trade but also a direct American
presence in foreign countries. Spokesmen for a stronger navy and
merchant marine, such as Theodore Roosevelt and Alfred T. Mahan,
saw Cuba both as evidence for their position and as an opportunity
to be exploited. A swelling sense of national pride, a rekindled faith
in Manifest Destiny, and a belief that the United States should take
its place among the shapers of world affairs combined to give the
Cuban crisis an immediacy that would have been improbable ten
years before.

Partisan politics made the Cuban question inescapable. For the
Democrats, split by free silver and the agonies of the Cleveland

administration, sympathy for the rebels might provide the means of regaining power from the GOP. Before the Philippine issue emerged, the Democracy was interventionist. Recognition of Cuban belligerency, said Ohio Democrats in 1897, was "an act of justice to an American nation struggling for liberty against foreign oppression."[5] The Republicans had long been more expansionist-minded than their rivals, and substantial elements within the party favored taking strong action against Spain. A number of conservative, influential Republican senators, however, worried over the effect that a war would have on the economy; so they counseled restraint. But neither major party could afford to let the other have the credit for chastising Spain and freeing Cuba. In Spain, no government could continue if it publicly accepted the loss of Cuba; in the United States, no administration could succeed politically if it was perceived as being pro-Spanish. Within those irreconcilable assumptions, Grover Cleveland and William McKinley operated from 1895 to 1898.

Grover Cleveland dealt with the Cuban issue for more than two years, and his policy and McKinley's are usually depicted as being continuous and similar. In fact, their approaches differed fundamentally on one essential point: Cleveland and his secretary of state, Richard Olney, pursued a course that was pro-Spanish; McKinley tilted toward the rebels. The Cleveland administration believed that the maintaining of Spanish sovereignty over Cuba was preferable to having an independent island whose consequent internal turmoil might lead to European intervention. The continuation of Spanish rule was also better than having America annex Cuba. Cleveland sought to obtain reforms from Spain for the Cubans, but always within the framework of the hegemony of Madrid.

In pursuit of these goals, President Cleveland opposed in 1896 repeated congressional efforts to accord belligerent rights to the Cubans or to recognize their independence. He did his best to enforce neutrality laws against filibustering to Cuba. For a time in 1895 Secretary Olney edged away from an anti-Cuban posture, but his tolerance for the insurgent cause ebbed in early 1896. He came to believe that the junta was merely a propaganda agency, that the rebellion was resulting in the destruction of property, and that Cuban independence would lead to a racial war. After Congress adjourned in April 1896, Cleveland and Olney proposed to the Spanish that their two countries cooperate "in the immediate pacification of the island on such a plan as, leaving Spain her rights of sovereignty, shall yet secure to the people of the island all such rights and powers of local self-government as they can reasonably ask."[6] That this idea would have had little support in Congress and no hope of acceptance in Cuba seemed not to have entered Cleveland's thinking.

The Spanish declined Cleveland's proposals. They pointed out that the rebels would not countenance mediation, and they concluded that "there is no effectual way to pacify Cuba unless it begins with the actual submission of the armed rebels to the mother country."[7] In the summer of 1896 Madrid sought to offset any kind of American action on Cuba by forming a coalition of European powers that would restrain the United States. This strategy, to which Spain would return, came to little when the American minister obtained a copy of the memorandum on which the effort relied. To the informal overtures that Spain made after the United States had protested, most of the nations that were approached made polite, noncommital responses.

Despite these rebuffs, the Cleveland administration persisted in its attempt to work out a negotiated settlement that would perpetuate Spanish control. For Spain a prolonged diplomatic interchange was in line with its policy of procrastination. Among the ideas discussed were a commercial treaty, which would set out reforms, or some form of Cuban autonomy. A presidential emissary went to the island in 1896/1897 to determine whether the rebels would accept autonomy. They would not.

It is in light of these ongoing activities that Cleveland's annual message of December 7, 1896, must be evaluated. During his discussion of Cuba, the president noted: "It can not be reasonably assumed that the hitherto expectant attitude of the United States will be indefinitely maintained. While we are anxious to accord all due respect to the sovereignty of Spain, we can not view the pending conflict in all its features, and properly apprehend our inevitably close relations to it, and its possible results, without considering that by the course of events we may be drawn into such an unusual and unprecedented condition, as will fix a limit to our patient waiting for Spain to end the contest, either alone and in her own way, or with our friendly cooperation."

These comments, in addition to Cleveland's remark that "the United States is not a nation to which peace is a necessity," have been taken as a warning to Spain that America would intervene if reforms did not occur.[8] More plausibly, the administration wanted to have the Spanish immediately grant reforms that would form the basis for the rebels to accept autonomy. To make that possible, the message had to preempt any congressional action on Cuban independence that might cause the rebels to reject autonomy. Cleveland's words did not foreshadow a lessening of his pro-Spanish stance. They constituted a diplomatic maneuver designed to safeguard his domestic flank while negotiations on autonomy continued.

When Cleveland left office, the nation had no viable Cuban policy. The president and Olney had repelled the most recent congressional attempt to recognize Cuban belligerency in December 1896. They had tried to find a solution within the framework of Spanish sovereignty, a course that allowed Madrid ample time to try a military solution on the island. The Cleveland administration prevented war for two years, but it did so through policies of endorsing Spanish dominance and of opposing the rebels, which fewer and fewer Americans accepted. There was little in Cleveland's actions to persuade Spain that time was running out in Cuba. The belief in Madrid that Spain might procrastinate with some hope of success would be an important obstacle to McKinley's new program of escalating pressure on the Spanish to give up their most important remaining possession in the western hemisphere.

The comparative calm in Spanish-American relations in the spring of 1897 gave the new president a period in which to shape his Cuban policy. Between March and May the administration had only to deal with such long-standing but comparatively minor issues as the status of Cuban prisoners in Spanish jails, filibustering, and losses of American property. During its special session on the tariff, Congress also turned to Cuba. In mid May the Senate passed a resolution to recognize the belligerent rights of the rebels; but it died in the House, where Speaker Thomas B. Reed bottled it up. The question of suffering among American citizens in Cuba arose in the Senate debate, and the ensuing inquiry led to a presidential message in which he sought $50,000 for relief of these individuals. Congress responded affirmatively later in May. "The policy of the Administration in reference to Cuba," said the *New York Tribune*, "is not likely to be criticised, as was that of its predecessor, on the score of vacillation or indifference to the rights of American citizens."[9]

McKinley's policy on the larger questions concerning Cuba emerged slowly. He made some overtures to Spain about selling the island, but received a negative response. With that option temporarily closed, the administration sought hard, reliable information about Cuba. The consul in Havana, Fitzhugh Lee, was a Cleveland appointee who favored intervention and was prorebel in his reports and public statements. Cleveland and Olney had distrusted him, and suspicions about his reliability persisted. To remove Lee, however, might suggest a repudiation of his views. Instead, the president decided to send to Cuba a personal representative on whose judgment he could rely.

McKinley first looked to his old friend William R. Day. As Secretary Sherman's mental weaknesses became apparent, however, Day was named assistant secretary of state in late April. The Canton attorney was just forty-eight years old when he came to Washington. Though he liked to style himself as just a country lawyer, his firm of Lynch and Day was one of Canton's most prosperous. Day had known McKinley since the early 1870s and had acted as an advisor to his friend in the 1893 fund episode, in the 1896 campaign, and in forming his cabinet. Discreet and controlled, the balding, slight, mustachioed lawyer provided McKinley with reliable, temperate counsel; and reporters soon recognized Day as the real power in the State Department.

To replace Day on the fact-finding mission to Cuba, William J. Calhoun, an Illinois Republican who was an associate of Charles G. Dawes, left in early May and spent almost four weeks on a tour of the devastated island. His report, submitted on June 22, 1897, led to the McKinley government's first overt statement to Spain. Calhoun found Cuba, under Weyler's reconcentration policy, "wrapped in the stillness of death and the silence of desolation." He held out little hope that Spain could reestablish its hold, that autonomy could work, or that independence for Cuba would be feasible.[10] With Calhoun's comments before him, the president informed the Spanish minister on June 26 that warfare in Cuba "shall at least be conducted according to the military codes of civilization." McKinley had articulated one of the central points of his policy toward Spain. The United States had a right to insist that the suppression of the rebellion be carried on within humane limits and that Spain not use "fire and famine to accomplish by uncertain indirection what the military arm seems powerless to directly accomplish." Spain did not accept the American position, but McKinley remained adamant that his government could monitor Spanish conduct.[11]

If dealing with the Cuban problem required clear information from the scene, it also demanded that there be an American minister in Madrid in whom the president had confidence. During the spring, McKinley approached John W. Foster, Henry White, Whitelaw Reid, Elihu Root, Jacob D. Cox, and Seth Low, who was then president of Columbia University, about the office. For personal reasons or because of the difficulty of the position, all declined.

McKinley told Low that he "was desirous to adopt every possible measure to bring about a change" in Spanish-American relations before Congress assembled in December, "when it would be necessary for him to define his 'policy.'" Opposing annexation because "the U.S. would not know what to do with the island," McKinley added that "if nothing could be done with Spain, he desired to be able to show that we had spared no effort to avert trouble." Finally, in late June, Stewart L. Woodford, an able lawyer who had been a Civil War general and lieutenant governor of New York in the 1860s, agreed to go to Madrid. The sixty-one-year-old Woodford was loyal and conscientious, but the subtleties of international diplomacy would test his abilities in 1897/1898.[12]

In the last half of 1897, relations between Spain and the United States improved as Madrid made concessions over Cuba; and Washington apparently achieved results that justified McKinley's diplomatic methods. A change in the Spanish government was the largest single cause of this temporary rapprochement. The ruling Conservative party was under heavy assault for its failure to quell the Cuban uprising. The Liberals called for autonomy and a political settlement. On August 8, 1897, the Conservative prime minister, Antonio Canovas del Castillo, was assassinated. An interim Conservative government, which held office during August and September, replied to McKinley's note of June 26. The document, delivered on August 26, rebutted McKinley's strictures on the war in Cuba. What the Spanish had done was no worse than the way the Union army had functioned in the American Civil War, Madrid said.

Two months after Canovas's death, a Liberal government, with Praxedes M. Sagasta at its head, took power. In its first cabinet meeting, the new regime decided to recall General Weyler and to offer the Cubans some form of autonomy. To Sagasta and his associates, a policy of appeasing the United States and seeking a negotiated peace with the rebels seemed to be the most promising way of resolving Spain's internal problems without doing serious damage to the nation. In a newspaper interview, however, the prime minister noted that "no Spanish party, certainly not the Liberals, could assent to foreign interference in our domestic affairs or with our colonies."[13]

While Spain passed through its political crisis, the new American minister explored official opinion in London and Paris before reaching Madrid on September 1. Three weeks after arriving in Spain, Woodford met with the foreign minister on September 18, 1897, and delivered to the Spanish the diplomatic initiatives of the

McKinley administration. McKinley had drafted the formal instructions that Woodford carried, a document that established the framework of the president's policy through the outbreak of war. Spain must, if it could, subdue the rebellion within a limited period of time. Protracted fighting brought "upon the United States a degree of injury and suffering which can not longer be ignored." The administration hoped, however, that the Spanish would accept the inevitable and consider "whether the time has not arrived when Spain . . . will put a stop to this destructive war" by offering "proposals of settlement honorable to herself and just to her Cuban colony and to mankind." If Madrid did not do this, McKinley was convinced that, "should his present effort be fruitless, his duty to his countrymen will necessitate an early decision as to the course of action which the time and the transcendent emergency may demand." Woodford repeated these remarks in September, adding the requirement that he receive an answer by November 1.[14]

McKinley did not say at the outset that Spain must relinquish Cuba, but his skepticism about a military solution reflected his lack of confidence in Spanish arms. Since the president would not make an arrangement that would be unacceptable to the rebels, the plain thrust of his policy was to induce Spain, by incremental steps and intensifying diplomatic pressure, to yield Cuba without going to war. Since Americans believed that abandonment of the island would be in Spain's best interest, it was logical to assume that, given enough time, Spain would assess the problem in the same way. The premise that Spain would eventually recognize the wisdom of peaceful submission lay at the heart of McKinley's strategy.

The Sagasta government was able to make positive gestures in apparent response to the American requests. On October 23, 1897, Woodford was told that the decrees granting autonomy to Cuba would soon be issued. During the next month the Spanish suspended the reconcentration policy, declared an amnesty for political prisoners, and released Americans who were in Cuban jails. On November 25 the autonomy plan was announced. It gave Cuba a greater degree of home rule than ever before, but it left Spanish sovereignty over military and foreign affairs intact. In late November an administration official told reporters: "Thus far Spain has surrendered everything asked of her, and the policy of the administration has been completely vindicated." McKinley knew of the shortcomings of the autonomy plan, but clearly he hoped that an affirmative answer to the Spanish actions would impel further concessions.[15]

The president's annual message on December 6, 1897, reflected the administration's desire to give the Spanish reforms a chance to work, while simultaneously maintaining the diplomatic pressure that had operated to that point. "The Government of Sagasta has entered upon a course from which recession with honor is impossible," McKinley said, adding that Spain deserved "a reasonable chance to realize her expectations and to prove the asserted efficacy of the new order of things to which she stands irrevocably committed." There was an implied time limit in other words of the message: "The near future will demonstrate whether the indispensable condition of a righteous peace, just alike to the Cubans and to Spain as well as equitable to all our interests so intimately involved in the welfare of Cuba, is likely to be attained. If not, the exigency of further and other action by the United States will remain to be taken."[16]

Because the message came out against the recognition of Cuban belligerency, the more strident champions of the rebels assailed it. The Democratic caucus in the House resolved in favor of recognizing that "a condition of war exists in the island of Cuba between the Government of Spain and the Cuban people." The Spanish government, which was more concerned with the morale of the rebels, reading the message for clues about how their enemies might react, bridled at the president's cautionary words. An American army officer in Madrid wrote: "The President's message has been received in a spirit of intense hostility by everyone except the Cabinet of Sagasta, and the unofficial expressions of some of its members are by no means friendly. They see in it a veiled threat of intervention unless war in Cuba stops. And against that all Spain is one."[17]

The first and most productive phase of McKinley's Cuban diplomacy ended in December 1897. Spain had conceded much, and public opinion in the United States seemed to be inclined to support McKinley. Additional progress, of course, depended on the effective operation of Spain's program regarding autonomy. In December the president looked for signs of success but took precautions against failure. With suffering still prevalent on the island, the White House made successive appeals on Christmas Eve, 1897, and January 8, 1898, for donations to the Red Cross. McKinley himself contributed five thousand dollars anonymously. On the military side, the navy was instructed to have the North Atlantic squadron conduct winter maneuvers in the Caribbean near Key West. The battleship *Maine* had already been ordered to that Florida port, and the Navy discussed contingency plans for sending a ship to Havana.

More ominously, on January 11, 1898, the secretary of the navy directed the commander of the European Squadron to retain sailors whose enlistments were about to run out. These orders were part of McKinley's strategy to convince Spain that the United States was not bluffing over Cuba. Behind the military decisions of these months was the directing hand of the president.

Changes in the international situation at the end of 1897 and in the early weeks of 1898 underscored the desirability of a prompt resolution of the Cuban question. In Asia the actions of European powers to gain military and economic concessions from China, which was symbolized by the German occupation of Kiaochow Bay in November 1897, troubled an administration that was interested in the expansion of trade in the Far East. Beyond involving the fate of Cuba itself, the instability in the Caribbean that grew out of strained Spanish-American relations could tempt other nations to challenge the long-term ascendancy of the United States in the area. When Germany used gunboat diplomacy against Haiti in December, the administration watched events closely. Two months later the navy sent a high-ranking officer, Arent S. Crowninshield, to visit Santo Domingo and then report on German penetration. "I do not hesitate to predict," he wrote, "that before many years have passed, Germany will succeed in acquiring one or more territorial possessions in the Western Hemisphere." Until a satisfactory end to the controversy with Spain could be achieved, however, these foreign-policy concerns would mark time.[18]

Spain's autonomy program for Cuba went into effect on January 1, 1898. Fitzhugh Lee wired the State Department eleven days later: "Mobs, led by Spanish officers, attacked to-day the offices of the four newspapers here advocating autonomy." These outbreaks, in which the pro-Spanish rioters cried, "Death to autonomy," convinced McKinley that Spain could not make its colonial reforms work. The Spanish minister told his superiors that the administration seemed to have lost all faith in Spain's success. The January 12 riots marked the beginning of the rapid deterioration in relations that exposed the irreconcilable differences between Spain and the United States over Cuba.[19]

The Havana disturbances revived congressional interest in the recognition of Cuban belligerency. For the next week, House Democrats assailed the administration as being pro-Spanish. The Republicans repulsed these challenges, but the debates revealed the shrinking limits of McKinley's options. "The President, while he does not favor the recognition of belligerency as a specific cure or as advisable, has intimated where the line of duty will take him, acting not by halves, but facing the whole question," said an administration spokesman in the House. The British ambassador, Sir Julian Paunce-fote, reported "a feeling of disquietude and alarm" at what were deemed to be semiofficial comments.[20]

The attacks of the opposition, the prospect of injury to Americans in Cuba, and the need to impress Madrid also persuaded the White House that it was desirable to send an American ship to Havana. Such an act required Spain's agreement, and it appeared at first as though Dupuy de Lôme and his government, eager as they were to discredit Consul Lee, would refuse. On January 20 the Spanish minister characterized the sending of American vessels to the island as an unfriendly act. Four days later, however, in an interview with Secretary Day, Dupuy de Lôme learned that the president was inclined to give autonomy a little more time in which to work. Since Spain believed that it was already working, because "Spain and the United States were at peace," McKinley wanted to resume the navy's visits to Cuban ports.[21]

When Dupuy replied that discontinuance of the visits had not been a proper thing to do, the administration acted that same day to order the *Maine* to Havana. On January 25 the battleship "came gliding into the harbor as easily and smoothly as possible." At a diplomatic dinner the next day, McKinley sought out Dupuy publicly and said: "I see that we have only good news; I am well satisfied with what has occurred in the House, and with the discipline of the Republicans. You, who comprehend this, will understand how strong our position is and how much it has changed and bettered in the past year; you have no occasion to be other than satisfied and confident."[22]

The actual course of relations over the next two weeks belied these optimistic assertions. In Spain the prowar forces gained a temporary ascendancy. Reinforcements for Cuba were readied, and purchases of ammunition went forward. The navy began negotiations to acquire additional ships from Great Britain and several Latin American nations, repairs were rushed on Spain's larger vessels, and planners drafted operational strategies for use in North American waters. On the American side the navy stepped up its drive for greater readiness. Major commands were warned of possible trouble with Spain, and ships gathered intelligence about conditions in Cuban harbors where landings might be made.

The sterner mood in Madrid also shaped its response to American diplomatic actions at the end of 1897. On December 20

Woodford gave the Spaniards the administration's reply to the Sagasta ministry's statements and actions of October. The note said of the autonomy program: "In taking this advanced position the Government of Spain has entered upon a pathway from which no backward step is possible." The Spanish answer, given to Woodford on February 1, 1898, took a very hard line toward McKinley's assumption that the United States could monitor Spain's handling of autonomy or set implicit deadlines for its effectiveness to be established. "It is only in this formula of colonial self-government and Spanish sovereignty that peace, which is so necessary to the Peninsula and to Cuba and so advantageous to the United States, can be found." About foreign intrusion or interference, the Spanish concluded that "such interference would lead to an intervention which any nation possessing any self respect would have to repel by force, even if it were necessary to exhaust, in the defense of the integrity of its territory and of its independence, all, absolutely all, the resources at its disposal." Woodford was handed the note on February 3, but because of slowness in translating it, a cable did not go to the State Department until February 8. The wire reached the president the next day.[23]

Two incidents, successive and sensational, now lifted the Cuban problem beyond diplomacy and placed it at the center of public attention. In mid December, Dupuy de Lôme wrote a personal letter to a friend in Cuba that characterized McKinley as "weak and a bidder for the admiration of the crowd, besides being a would-be politician who tries to leave a door open behind himself while keeping on good terms with the jingoes of his party." The letter fell into the hands of the Cubans, they sent it to the junta in New York, and the *New York Journal* published it on February 9, 1898. For Dupuy it meant the end of his career, as the administration insisted on an apology from Spain in addition to his resignation. The yellow journals made the most of this "Worst Insult to the United States in Its History," and in Congress there was a renewed demand that the consular correspondence on conditions in Cuba be published. To this last request, which came to a head by February 14, the administration gave its tacit assent.

McKinley's willingness to make such a move in the direction of war, for the reports would only arouse congressional ire toward Spain, testified to the true importance of the de Lôme letter. The president brushed aside the insult to himself and instead focused on a concluding paragraph in the letter. "It would be very advantageous," Dupuy de Lôme had said, "to take up, even if only for effect, the question of commercial relations, and to have a man of some prominence sent hither in order that I may make use of him here to carry on a propaganda among the Senators and others in opposition to the junta and to try to win over the refugees." For some weeks, Madrid had been discussing a commercial treaty of reciprocity. It now seemed clear that Spain was stalling. Coupled with the note of February 1, the de Lôme letter made the chances of avoiding war slight, even before a fresh disaster overtook the two nations.[24]

About one-thirty on the morning of February 16, 1898, Secretary of the Navy Long received a dispatch from Lee that began: "*Maine* blown up and destroyed to-night at 9:40 p. m." Long sent Commander D. W. Dickens to the White House with the news. Dickens later recalled: "The President came out in his dressing gown. I handed him the despatch which he read with great gravity. He seemed to be very deeply impressed with the news, handed back the despatch to me, and took it again, two or three times, expressing great regret that the event had happened, particularly at that time." Two hundred and sixty-four enlisted men and two officers had perished. The nation instinctively asked, as McKinley did of Dickens, how the accident could have occurred, and there was an immediate disposition to blame Spain for, at best, carelessness or, at worst, conspiracy.[25]

The most modern study of the destruction of the *Maine* argues persuasively that it was caused accidentally by an internal explosion. Since it used bituminous coal as fuel, the ship was vulnerable to spontaneous combustion from its inadequately ventilated bunkers. Heat from the ensuing fire set off the gunpowder in an adjacent reserve magazine. The problems that faced William McKinley on the morning of February 16 were how to respond to this catastrophe, how to determine the cause of the explosion, and how to maintain control of the diplomatic situation. Long told the press immediately, at the president's behest, that "judgment should be suspended until a full investigation is made." Meanwhile, the administration moved toward a greater preparation for hostilities, launched a court of inquiry into the sinking, and resumed the effort to induce Spain to yield. The White House knew that the report of the naval board set an implied deadline for additional action. For the most part, McKinley remained quiet, with only an oblique public reference to the crisis. Speaking on Washington's Birthday in Philadelphia, he reviewed the career of the first president and remarked that "the exercise of a sober and dispassionate public

Wreckage of the *Maine* in Havana Harbor. Photography
Collection, Humanities Research Center, University of
Texas at Austin

judgment [was] the best safeguard in the calm of tranquil events, and rises superior and triumphant above the storms of woe and peril."[26]

Public opinion, of course, was much less temperate than was McKinley. The *Denver News* observed that the withdrawal of Spain from this side of the Atlantic would be a proper atonement for the *Maine*. Spaniards were hanged in effigy in numerous communities, and the French ambassador found that "a sort of bellicose fury has seized the American nation." For all the frenzy, however, the country accepted the decision that no definite action should occur until the naval board had reported.[27]

Critics of McKinley have identified the period just after the destruction of the *Maine* as a time when he should have rallied the public against war with Spain. But what could he have said? His diplomacy depended on convincing Spain to accept the loss of Cuba without making a public demand that she give up the island. Therefore, he could not make public his intentions without drawing a negative Spanish response that would bring war closer. In advance of the report, a comment that the explosion was accidental and that Spain was blameless would have risked an embarrassing repudiation. To say that the United States would not fight over Cuba was politically impossible. Peace was feasible if either Spain or the United States would modify its position; but as the next five weeks proved, this did not happen.

For the Spanish, this period revealed the limited options that confronted them. The warlike mood of the Spanish government in late January abated in the wake of the *Maine* episode, America's military preparations, and an awareness of Spain's own naval weakness. To find a solution short of war, the queen regent discussed the possibility of selling Cuba but found that the army was opposed to such a humiliation. Alternatively, the Sagasta ministry revived the idea of holding peace talks with the rebels. The need to mollify the army, however, meant that the insurgents had to request an armistice before negotiations could begin. Unsuccessful in appeasing the United States because of domestic opposition and unwilling to face war as a diversion from its internal problems, the Spanish government could only hope that support from its European allies would stave off war over Cuba.

The McKinley administration devoted this interval to renewing the pressure on Spain and to intensifying the military preparations for a possible outbreak of fighting. The president once again explored the possibility of purchasing Cuba as well as alternative governmental arrangements for the island. His most dramatic action was to call congressional leaders to the White House in early March, when he asked one of them, Joseph G. Cannon of Illinois, to introduce a bill appropriating $50 million for national defense. A Spanish naval build-up had worried American officials since the early part of the year. "Month by month the Spanish Navy has been put into a better condition to meet us," wrote Theodore Roosevelt on February 16. When the press reported on March 5 that the Spanish were discussing the purchase of two Brazilian cruisers under construction in England, McKinley acted.[28]

Within two days the president had his appropriation. Both houses passed it unanimously. The administration promptly used the money to obtain the two Brazilian ships before Spain could do so. Woodford reported that news that the defense bill had been passed had "simply stunned" the Spanish because it provided evidence of the ample material resources of the United States.[29]

While he awaited the report on the *Maine*, McKinley balanced the conflicting pressures from the parties in the Cuban imbroglio. The insurgents proposed on March 1 to pay Spain an indemnity of no more than $100 million in exchange for American and Spanish recognition of Cuba's independence and for the withdrawal of all Spanish troops. They assured the president: "We do not ask you to go to war; we only ask for your neutrality, for the recognition of Cuban belligerent rights." They did not explain how war with Spain could be averted after recognition was granted. Renewed discussions within the United States and with potential European intermediaries about possible purchase of the island found little domestic support and, in the end, resolute opposition in Spain.[30]

McKinley also looked briefly into an arrangement—drawn from the precedent of relations between Turkey and Egypt—in which Spain would keep not only a token sovereignty over the island but also some share of its customs revenues. When he examined the proposal with its author, Oscar Straus, a New York businessman, McKinley predicted: "We will have great trouble in satisfying the insurgents or in getting them to agree to anything—they are even more difficult than Spain to deal with." His forecast proved to be correct. The rebels rejected the plan quickly.[31]

Efforts to reach a settlement with Madrid in these weeks also proved fruitless. The Spanish wanted to consider America's support for Cuban autonomy, the recall of Lee from Havana, and movements of the United States Navy in the area. They made clear their lack of interest in selling Cuba, and they renewed their strategy of

Cartoon from *Judge*, March 26, 1898

delay when the Cortes, the Spanish parliament, adjourned in late February until April 25. On March 19 Woodford asked Washington to set April 15 as a deadline. "They should see that the United States mean business, and mean it *now*."[32]

Events in the third week of March 1898 now surged toward an American ultimatum to Spain. As the days passed, the expectation increased that the verdict on the *Maine* would put the blame on Spain. The tense popular mood became more heated on March 17 when Senator Redfield Proctor of Vermont described to his colleagues his conclusions formed from a recent trip to Cuba. His calm, matter-of-fact analysis made a deep impression. He found "the entire native population of Cuba, struggling for freedom and deliverance from the worst misgovernment of which I ever had knowledge." The result of the Spanish campaign, he decided, was "neither peace nor war. It is concentration and desolation." Proctor's remarks captured the popular mind. To hear his speech, said Senator Francis E. Warren of Wyoming, produced "a raising of the blood and temper as well as of shame that we, a civilized people, an enlightened nation, a great republic, born in a revolt against tyranny, should permit such a state of things within less than a hundred miles of our shore as that which exists in Cuba."[33]

In the march of public opinion toward an acceptance of war, Proctor's speech marked an important milestone. Among religious newspapers the belief that intervention could be justified on moral grounds, already a pervasive conviction, became even more widespread. Of equal, or perhaps more, significance was a shift in business attitudes. From a general stance against intervention, the business community joined the rest of the nation in a greater readiness to advocate hostilities.

As the most serious national crisis since the Civil War deepened, McKinley became the object of intense and simultaneous feelings of confidence, hope, mistrust, and disgust. "The President is behaving with great dignity and apparent firmness," wrote loyal Republican Senator John Coit Spooner, while the *Nation*, not normally a friendly journal, observed that "the American people no longer fear the executive, and they no longer trust the legislative body." The dominant critical note toward the president was that he might be too reluctant or timid to act with firmness toward Spain. His enemies alleged that his closeness to business, to "the clientele of wealth who are the holders of Spanish bonds," might dispose him to accept a peaceful solution that would be favorable to the oppressors of Cuba; and theater audiences jeered at McKinley's picture in

New York.[34] The tensions surrounding the coming of war were also preparing challenges to the president's control of foreign policy and of his own government.

For the man in the White House, the approach of spring brought only mounting personal anxiety. The attempt to restrain domestic agitation for war while inducing the Spanish to submit over Cuba taxed McKinley's physical resources. George B. Cortelyou found him, in late March, looking "quite well considering the enormous strain he is under, although for the past two or three days he has looked haggard at times." Visitors throughout these days heard him say: "I pray God that we may be able to keep peace," or as he had earlier remarked to Leonard Wood: "I shall never get into a war until I am sure that God and man approve. I have been through one war; I have seen the dead piled up; and I do not want to see another." While McKinley displayed, in this period, "a good deal of weariness and nervous strain," memoir accounts that have him in tears and despair seem, aside from the factual errors that they contain, to be unreliable in substance.[35]

The climactic phase of the Cuban problem began on March 19, 1898, when four members of the *Maine* inquiry board met with McKinley. They told him that the court would conclude that an external explosion, probably a submarine mine, had caused the *Maine* to sink. The physical evidence regarding the vessel's keel and bottom plates, which had been driven upward, as an explosion from outside would do, persuaded the court to reject the hypothesis of an internal explosion. Knowing that the court's verdict would have a profound influence on the popular mind when the report officially reached him four or five days later, McKinley sent a stern message to Woodford on March 20, which conveyed the board's findings and warned: "This report must go to Congress soon." The president indicated that the *Maine* issue could be handled through a payment of reparations by Spain, but "general conditions in Cuba which can not be longer endured, and which will demand action on our part," required positive steps in Madrid. "April 15 is none too early date for accomplishment of these purposes." At home, McKinley began a round of meetings with congressional leaders of both parties to offset the impact of the *Maine* report and to retain control of events. He agreed that Congress would receive diplomatic papers on Cuba by April 20, but still, in the face of a deadline for Spain and Congress, he hoped "that something may yet happen to avert hostilities." On the day that these words appeared in the *New York Herald*, the spiral into war commenced.[36]

41

The *Maine* report, blaming an external cause, arrived at the White House during the evening of March 24. The next day the president, the cabinet, and some military advisors digested the lengthy document. The report, with a message from McKinley, would go to Capitol Hill on Monday, March 28. Meanwhile, McKinley prepared a message to Woodford, which went out over Day's signature shortly after midnight on March 26. This telegram briefly reviewed McKinley's policy and then stated: "The President suggests that if Spain will revoke the reconcentration order and maintain the people until they can support themselves and offer to the Cubans full self-government, with reasonable indemnity, the President will gladly assist in its consummation. If Spain should invite the United States to mediate for peace and the insurgents would make like request, the President might undertake such office of friendship." Woodford received the wire late on March 26 and immediately asked if "full self-government" meant "actual recognition of independence, or is nominal Spanish sovereignty over Cuba still permissible?" Day responded that "full self-government with indemnity would mean Cuban independence."[37]

By Sunday, March 27, the president apparently had decided that Congress would not act hastily on the *Maine* report. At the same time, Woodford was reporting that Spain had made tentative feelers toward an armistice in Cuba. With the prospect of a slight breathing space, McKinley had Day wire the American minister: "See if the following can be done: First. Armistice until October 1. Negotiations meantime looking for peace between Spain and insurgents through friendly offices of President United States." Second, the president sought the revocation of the reconcentration order. Finally, Woodford was told to add, if possible, that if peace terms between Spain and the rebels were not reached by October 1, McKinley would be the final arbiter between the parties.[38]

McKinley's second proposal offered Spain a more measured path toward Cuban independence, but both the March 26 and the March 27 messages assumed, as an end result, a Cuba that would be free of Spanish rule. There was no outright demand for independence, because the Spanish government would have peremptorily rejected it. Imprecision in diplomacy would offer a slim chance to avoid war, if Spain were to yield. Categorical ultimatums at any point in the negotiating process would have meant hostilities.

In Madrid, Woodford submitted the American proposals to Spain on March 29. Faced with intense congressional pressure after McKinley's *Maine* message, the administration wanted a prompt response. Thursday, March 31, became the deadline. The Sagasta government found that the Spanish army was opposed to an armistice, and Woodford reported that the tender of an armistice would cause a revolution. In its formal answer, Spain agreed to submit the *Maine* question to arbitration and revoked the reconcentration order. On McKinley's principal demands, however, it yielded nothing. The Cuban problem would be turned over to that island's parliament, "without whose intervention it will not be able to arrive at the final result." Spain would accept an armistice if the rebels asked for it, but its length and extent would be up to the Spanish commander in Cuba. Spain had gone to the limit of its domestic political resources, but Cuban independence, either immediately through submission or eventually through American mediation, was an impossibility. Madrid was now seeking time in order to mobilize European support against the United States.[39]

For McKinley, events in Washington were eroding his flexibility in carrying out negotiations. His message about the *Maine* was low-key and calm. He predicted that "the sense of justice of the Spanish nation" would resolve the issue that the destruction of the vessel had posed, and he promised to advise Congress of the results. "In the meantime," the president concluded, "deliberate consideration is invoked." The message, said a *New York Herald* reporter, "fell like a wet blanket on Congress"; and Cortelyou noted in his diary on March 29 that "the feeling in Congress today is not so good as it was."[40] In the Senate, members introduced resolutions demanding that Spain withdraw from Cuba and authorizing the president to use force to compel Spain to comply with American demands. While these resolutions commanded wide support, the Republican leadership would not embarrass the White House by taking them up. On the House side the Democrats offered resolutions to recognize Cuban independence, which, in the wake of McKinley's message, attracted many Republicans. Their rebellion, which grew out of an informal GOP caucus on March 29, culminated the next day in bitter procedural struggles over a resolution dealing with recognition. It took not only the exertions of Speaker Reed but also a presidential promise of a message on Cuba in order to defeat the recognition forces. The issue now hung on Spain's answer to the March 26 and March 27 messages.

The negative reply reached the White House at 10:30 P.M. on March 31. Its unsatisfactory character was clear, and it left little room for additional negotiation. Without abandoning his hope that Spain might still recognize the necessity of relinquishing Cuba,

McKinley now moved to put the nation on a war footing. On April 1 the navy stepped up its preparations, including night patrols; the administration explored taxation problems that a war would bring; and the president began to work on his message to Congress. "That the President has less confidence in a peaceable outcome," wrote a reporter in the *New York Tribune* on April 1, "was apparent from the views he expressed to several of his closest friends." Congress expected to receive the message on April 4, and influential Republicans wanted the president to "lead and not be pushed." Then, on April 3, the White House announced that the message would go in two days later, on April 6.[41]

This brief delay may have been connected to a final presidential initiative to gain concessions from Spain. Through Archbishop John Ireland of Minnesota, an informal papal envoy, McKinley was exploring the prospects of having the Vatican use persuasion with Spain. The president's remark that he would welcome help from the Holy See meant that he wanted assistance in obtaining Spain's acquiescence. Madrid interpreted these words as an invitation to use papal mediation and as evidence of a relaxation of American pressure. Woodford received proposals that, in return for an armistice that Spain would grant, the United States would withdraw its navy from Cuban waters. He cabled Washington that "when armistice is once proclaimed hostilities will never be resumed and . . . permanent peace will be secured." The White House denied the Spanish interpretation as soon as it became public, and Day wired to Woodford: "Would the peace you are so confident of securing mean the independence of Cuba?" The more the administration learned of what Spain meant in its note of March 31, the less it liked the substance of it. The manifesto regarding the autonomous government, said Day on April 4, "is not armistice" but only "an invitation to the insurgents to submit," pending further Spanish action.[42]

On April 6, the anticipated date of McKinley's message, the morning began with "an immense crowd" of "more than ten thousand people" at the Capitol. About noon, however, McKinley received a dispatch from Lee: "If message can be withheld until Monday 11th can arrange everything. If sent before will have trouble here." The president called congressional leaders in and, in response to suggestions that the message be submitted anyway, said: "I will not do it; I will not send in that message today; I will not do such a thing if it will endanger the life of an American in Cuba." The lawmakers had "nothing to do but consent" to the five-day's postponement.[43]

For all the drama of Lee's plea on behalf of the safety of
Americans, diplomatic maneuvers made the additional time useful
to McKinley. In late March, Spain had played its final card, the
intervention by its European neighbors and allies. Though the
American position had little support on the Continent, there was
even less disposition to challenge the United States openly. Wary
of European interference and concerned about maintaining a posture for peace, the president agreed to accept a statement from the
ambassadors in favor of a peaceful outcome. In consultation with
the British ambassador, Sir Julian Pauncefote, McKinley helped to
draft a note that the envoys of the six major powers presented to
him on April 6. They earnestly hoped "that further negotiations
will lead to an agreement which, while securing the maintenance of
peace, will afford all necessary guaranties for the reestablishment
of order in Cuba." In response, McKinley spoke of the good will
behind the note and expressed his desire for a settlement that would
end "the chronic condition of disturbance there." McKinley may
well have postponed the delivery of the message in order to avoid
upstaging the Europeans and to preserve diplomatic activity related
to it which was then under way in Spain.[44]
     In March and early April, in response to German initiatives,
Pope Leo XIII, who was sympathetic to Spain, indicated his readiness to serve as a mediator in the Spanish-American dispute. Out of
these talks came, in late March, a proposal for the pope to intercede
if Spain would grant Cuba its independence. The Sagasta government rejected this idea within a few days. The abortive mission of
Archbishop Ireland was a part of this papal action. Finally, on April
2 the Vatican proposed to request an armistice. A week later the
Spanish agreed, in an action that has been persistently misinter-
preted as a capitulation to McKinley's demands. There is, the
president's attackers charge, no better evidence of his fecklessness,
his weakness, his lack of courage. No incident, the indictment runs,
better illustrates his ranking as a mediocre president.
     Spain's decision to ask for a suspension of hostilities in Cuba,
not an armistice, was directed at the European powers rather than
at McKinley and Washington. Knowing that capitulation to the
Americans was politically impossible, the government saw the truce
as a negotiating ploy in its efforts to find foreign support. Even so,
there was strong opposition within the cabinet to a move that might
alienate the armed forces. Proponents contended that the suspension would buy time so that Cuba could be defended against the
United States. The cabinet deadlock ended on April 9, when the

queen arranged for the ambassadors of the European powers to call in Madrid, as they had in Washington. The diplomats favored an armistice, in the interests of peace, and Spain could now consent, to placate potential friends. Within the cabinet, advocates of the move stressed that it would not be a prelude to surrender, and they noted that the suspension of hostilities, instead of an armistice, would not involve recognizing the rebel regime.[45]

Woodford believed, as he wired the president, that "the present Government is going, and is loyally ready to go, as fast and as far as it can." A closer reading of Spain's statement, which reached McKinley on April 10, revealed the true character of this "capitulation." The Spanish commander in Cuba could determine how long and under what conditions hostilities would stop. The insurgents were offered autonomy, with "the franchise and liberties" extended to such an extent "that no motive or pretext is left for claiming any fuller measure thereof." Whatever changes might take place in autonomy would be "within the bounds of reason and of the national sovereignty." Spain also revoked its policy of reconcentration and offered to submit the *Maine* question to arbitration. Of American mediation, a true armistice, and Cuba's independence, Spain said nothing. To Day's inquiry about whether Spain would give Cuba its independence if the United States deemed it necessary, the minister in Washington said only no.[46]

McKinley's critics place less weight on these considerations; they contend that Spain, once the fighting stopped, could not have resumed the struggle. Time would have been on the side of a peaceful solution. Such a result was, of course, possible, but now remains only a might-have-been. It is doubtful, however, that the rebels would have accepted the suspension, and it is even more unlikely that Spanish opinion would have endorsed a move toward peace. Announcement of the suspension brought public disturbances in Madrid. More important, the passage of time, after an American diplomatic concession, would have strengthened not only the Spanish will to fight but also the military power at its disposal. The minister of war told the Cuban commander, for example, that the cabinet had opted for the suspension in order to remedy "a scarcity of resources with which to defend our indisputable rights."[47] The Spanish proposal was a last-minute diplomatic gambit that, from an American perspective, revived old questions about Madrid's good faith in the negotiating process.

The belief that Spain submitted rests on a misreading of the evidence and owes much to retrospective guilt about the impact which the war had on American history. The hypothetical scenario that has McKinley risking the prestige of his office, the future of his party, and what Americans saw as the nation's honor in exchange for a settlement of the Cuban issue without war is an attractive one. Its advocates must recognize, however, the greater likelihood that after placing these elements at risk, McKinley would have been confronted with Cuban opposition, a rebellion in Congress, and mounting indications that the Spanish had abused his good will and trust. The devastating effect that such a humiliation would have had on the presidency and the government should not be weighed lightly.

After the last message from Spain came to the White House on the morning of April 10, the administration decided to take no action beyond adding the information that it contained to the president's address on the situation in Cuba. The document had been ready for a week. Hearing it in a cabinet meeting on April 4, Secretary Long noted in his diary: "I suppose it is the best he can do; yet, it seems to me, the narrative which he makes the basis of his conclusion leads to a very different result from that which he reaches."[48] Long attributed the defects in the message to the president's fatigue and overwork. It was the product, in its preliminary drafts and data, of several hands, including those of his secretary John Porter, Assistant Secretary of State Alvey Adee, Attorney General John W. Griggs, and McKinley himself. In the end, the message was something less than a ringing affirmation of an American purpose to commence war with Spain, because the president was still engaged, in these final hours, in buying more time in which Spain might yet agree to end its rule in Cuba. The ambiguity and equivocation of the message may have sacrificed something in appearances in order to serve McKinley's continuing purposes of avoiding war and of achieving his diplomatic goals.

Congress listened to the message on April 11 "with intense interest and profound silence" as the clerks droned through its seven thousand words. It was not a call to arms. McKinley began with a historical narrative of the nation's involvement with the Cuban issue. He reviewed the negotiations with Spain up to the action of the Sagasta government on March 31 in response to his note of March 27. "With this last overture in the direction of immediate peace, and its disappointing reception by Spain, the Executive is brought to the end of his effort." The absence here of any reference to Cuban independence disturbed legislators who had been assured that the administration had demanded it of Spain. Once again, categorical assertion of this goal in a presidential statement would have ensured that Spain would reject it.[49]

McKinley next turned to what the United States should do. He came out against a recognition of Cuban belligerency that would "accomplish nothing toward the one end for which we labor—the instant pacification of Cuba and the cessation of the misery that afflicts the island." American recognition of the Cuban Republic's independence was also ruled out as not being necessary "in order to enable the United States to intervene and pacify the island. To commit this country now to the recognition of any particular government in Cuba might subject us to embarrassing conditions of international obligation toward the organization so recognized." When a government appeared "capable of performing the duties and discharging the functions of a separate nation," the United States could adjust its position.

At this point in his message, McKinley weighed the alternatives of intervention as an impartial neutral or as an ally, presumably of the Cubans. He chose the former course, setting out four reasons to justify the American action. Humanitarian grounds were listed first: "It is no answer to say that this is all in another country, belonging to another nation, and is therefore none of our business. It is specially our duty, for it is right at our door." The citizens of Cuba required protection that no government currently afforded them. Therefore, "the very serious injury to the commerce, trade, and business of our people," as well as "the wanton destruction of property and devastation of the island," constituted the third ground for action. Finally, "the present condition of affairs in Cuba is a constant menace to our peace, and entails upon this Government an enormous expense." The president cited the *Maine* as "a patent and impressive proof of a state of things in Cuba that is intolerable." After quoting from Presidents Grant and Cleveland on the Cuban question and from his own annual message in 1897, McKinley asserted: "In the name of humanity, in the name of civilization, in behalf of endangered American interests which give us the right and the duty to speak and to act, the war in Cuba must stop." That sentence produced a wave of applause in the House chamber.[50]

McKinley then asked the lawmakers to "authorize and empower the President to take measures to secure a full and final termination of hostilities between the Government of Spain and the people of Cuba." He also sought authority to establish a stable government in Cuba, and "to use the military and naval forces of the United States as may be necessary for these purposes." Following two paragraphs that closed the original version of the message came two more that alluded to Spain's suspension of hostilities. "If this measure attains a successful result," the president wrote, "then our aspirations as a Christian, peace-loving people will be realized. If it fails, it will be only another justification for our contemplated action."[51]

McKinley had not submitted a war message. The possibility of further negotiations with Spain remained alive, and the language about Cuba's belligerency and independence ensured that Congress would debate the issue for several days. The executive had also requested large discretionary power to use the nation's military force short of actually going to war. Even at this moment of greatest crisis for his administration, McKinley was broadening the scope of presidential power. The debate over the message in the next week would pivot on the issue of the president's leadership in the conduct of foreign policy and implicitly on his power as commander in chief.

Reaction to the message followed the broad outlines of public opinion on Cuba. Democrats called it "a great disappointment to the American people," and a warlike Republican, Foraker of Ohio, said: "I have no patience with the message, and you can say so." These early negative responses did not reflect the predominant evaluation of what McKinley had written. Secretary Cortelyou gave the president "opinions of the message as they have come in—both sides. There are not many of the critical kind notwithstanding statements made by members of Congress and others." Comments in the press and in the White House mail did indicate a broadly based support for what McKinley had done. For a message that has often been decried as being inconsistent, insipid, contradictory, or even turgid, it had a decisive effect in reclaiming the president's prestige at the end of a painful and protracted diplomatic controversy. It also succeeded in establishing the terms of the debate by which Congress took the nation into war with Spain.[52]

After McKinley's message, the Democrats planned their strategy around two issues—whether Cuban independence should be recognized and how much power the president should have in regard to foreign policy. At a Jefferson Day dinner on April 13, William Jennings Bryan came out for a government in Cuba "of such a character that one of our ships should not be blown up while under its protection," and a Democratic newspaper complained that the president "asks Congress to delegate its war-making power and all control over the crisis to him." On April 13, House Democrats offered a resolution to recognize the Cuban republic, but the Republican majority rejected it by 150 for to 190 against. That same day, language that the president endorsed was passed by the lopsided margin of 325 to 19. The resolution authorized and directed McKinley to intervene in order to end the war, called both for a stable and independent government for the Cuban people and for putting the land and naval forces of the nation behind the resolution.[53]

McKinley had obtained all that he wanted from the House, but the Senate advocates of war and Cuban independence were hardly satisfied. The Senate Foreign Relations Committee offered a resolution that was acceptable to the president, but Foraker drafted an amendment, which was introduced by Senator David Turpie of Indiana, that would have recognized the Cuban republic "as the true and lawful government of that island." This amendment gathered the backing of the Democrats, and eleven Republicans who were suspicious of McKinley, including Foraker and William E. Chandler, voted for it. Proponents of it contended that the president was scheming to avoid war and that he was trying to protect the holders of $500 million of Spanish bonds. McKinley's defenders replied that it would be "a grave mistake" to recognize Cuba "as an independent state among the nations of the world." On April 16 the amendment passed, 51 to 37. At this time the Senate also adopted an amendment offered by Senator Henry M. Teller of Colorado, according to which the United States would disavow any intention of controlling Cuba once hostilities had ceased. The final version of the Senate resolution, which passed by 67 to 21, contained the Foreign Relations Committee's language, Teller's amendment, and the Turpie-Foraker amendment.[54]

The problem for McKinley now lay in the House, where the vote on the Senate resolution was scheduled for Monday, April 18. During the weekend, administration spokesmen told reporters that the president might veto what the Senate had done if the House adopted it. Citing "several well-informed persons in authority," the *Washington Star* reported: "The President is ready to immediately put into execution by force of arms an intervention resolution of Congress, but he would be positive against any action which would usurp his prerogatives as he sees the matter." There were also hints that, once the fighting should start, recognition might be more feasible. On the eve of the vote it seemed that the antirecognition forces were in control. When Speaker Reed counted heads on Monday morning, however, the expected majority had disappeared.

Rapid parliamentary footwork recaptured the initiative, and the administration won by 178 to 156. The recognition forces held out in the Senate during the afternoon, but then conceded defeat. Finally, on April 19, resolutions that the president approved of passed the Senate by 7 votes and by 311 to 6 in the House. Congress, said one cabinet member, had come to a reasonable conclusion. McKinley had won and, in doing so, had "asserted the primacy of the President in foreign affairs at a time when either an independent-minded Congress or an inflamed public opinion might have inspired action that he deemed unwise."[55]

The president signed the congressional resolution on April 20. Spain broke diplomatic relations at once. In Madrid, Woodford was informed of Spain's action before he could convey the resolution formally, and he asked for his passports. On April 22 a naval blockade of Cuba was imposed, and two days later, Spain declared war as American ships moved into position. The action of their government was popular with the Spanish people, a response that underlined how little room there had actually been for carrying on negotiations over Cuba. On April 25 McKinley asked Congress to declare war, and it complied by passing a resolution that said that war had existed since April 21.

Of the two dominant explanations for McKinley's Spanish-Cuban diplomacy, the view that he was a weak, indecisive executive, who yielded at last to war hysteria, has commanded more adherents than the view that he was a wily expansionist, who in the end, wanted "what only a war could provide: the disappearance of the terrible uncertainty in American political and economic life, and a solid basis from which to resume the building of the new American commercial empire."[56] The first hypothesis assumes several considerations: that the Spanish would ultimately have submitted peacefully, that they virtually gave in, in April 1898, and that McKinley lacked the courage and vision to seize the real chances for peace. The evidence from Spanish diplomatic sources does not provide much support for the first two assumptions. Madrid did not see itself as being on a road from which no backward step was possible. With resolve and purpose, it maneuvered to maintain its grip on Cuba to the end, and its celebrated concessions of April 9, 1898, were, in fact, last-minute efforts to buy more time to keep the island.

The allegation of presidential weakness remains the most damning indictment of McKinley. When seen in the light of Spanish tenacity, however, what is remarkable is how long the president was able to obtain time for the conducting of peaceful diplomacy.

At any point in the process from November 1897 onward, the two countries were likely to begin fighting. Through this morass of crisis and danger, McKinley worked his way for five months in order to allow Spain the chance to submit peacefully. Finally, in April 1898, it was obvious that diplomacy had failed, that Spain would not yield, and that war was the only alternative to the prolongation of an intolerable foreign-policy situation. His conduct up to that point reveals a subtlety of action, a fortitude of will, and a simple courage that belie the easy stereotypes of his historical reputation.

The second school of McKinley's critics presents a more sophisticated bill of particulars. They question whether the motives behind the nation's concern with Cuba were genuine or whether they sprang from less attractive premises. Behind the stated reasons for American interest in Cuba lay economic causes—the tensions within a society that was emerging from a prolonged depression, an industrial machine that was glutted with its products and was seeking foreign markets, and statesmen who, unwilling to confront internal problems, preferred to export their social difficulties. The often unstated theses of this approach seem to be that the United States had, at most, marginal interests in the Cuban crisis beyond economic ones and that McKinley took his cues from the business community. On the latter point the image of the president as the tool of capitalists has confused the situation. McKinley operated within the framework of the economic system that he knew, in pursuit of the national interest of a society whose values, he thought, were basically healthy. He sought the counsel of successful businessmen on many issues, but the ostensible connections between their advice on Cuba and his actions remains ephemeral and inferential. Though the business community and its spokesmen responded to foreign policy, they did not make it.

It is possible to visualize Americans turning away from the horrors of the Cuban conflict, rejecting anything beyond the most modest role in foreign affairs, and addressing the society's inequities through some form of democratic socialism in 1898, but this is an improbable vision. The nation's historic traditions, humanitarian impulses, and economic calculations gave the Cuban problem a strong grip on the emotions of a majority of American citizens. It would have taken a revolution in attitudes, outside the existing political consensus, to have produced any other result than intense absorption in the fate of Cuba. To that foreign-policy commitment, Americans brought motives at once cynical and elevated, crass and noble. When economic causes are omitted, the picture lacks clarity, but excessive emphasis on them reduces foreign affairs to a crude equation that misreads the national character.

But was Cuba any business of the United States? Perhaps not; but it is hard to see how the effects of the rebellion could have been escaped. Few scholars advocate that the president should have joined Spain in suppressing the uprising. Another position contends that all the United States had to do was to recognize Cuba's independence, since the rebels had won militarily. Spain would have questioned whether the verdict on the war was that clear, and recognition would have meant war in any case, as 1898 showed. An independent Cuba, free from outside influence, is a laudable goal; and a unilateral defense of the American presence there during this century is difficult. It takes a great faith in the benevolent workings of international politics in these years, however, to maintain that Cuba would not, in the absence of United States involvement, have at least been the object of attention from nations such as Germany which had a larger capacity to assert their will than did Spain.

Like most wars, the Spanish-American War occurred when two nations, both convinced that they were right, pursued their national interests to an ultimate conclusion. Spain tried to defend its territorial integrity and sense of nationhood with the limited means open to it. In order to end a bloody conflict, the United States, under the leadership of William McKinley, went to war in 1898 against a foe that had resisted all attempts at peaceful compromise. The nation's motives owed far more to the better side of American life than posterity has recognized. If the war that ensued was not splendid, it had come in a way that dishonored neither the two countries involved nor the presidency of William McKinley.

3

THE PRESIDENT'S WAR

The war that the United States waged against Spain for a little more than three months in 1898 lingers in the national memory as a blend of farce, drama, and unexpected world responsibility. "Was there ever before such a war with such great results, so short in duration, such wonderful successes, with no reverses?" asked Senator Redfield Proctor three days after the fighting had stopped.[1] Yet, despite the abundant information on its military and diplomatic events, the war has not received very much attention as a force for social change at the end of the nineteenth century. There has been even less examination of what the war did to the presidential office under McKinley.

Men who were close to the White House agreed that William McKinley ran the war on the American side. "In all the movements of the army and navy the President's hand is seen," wrote Cortelyou in his diary. Charles Emory Smith offered a similar opinion after McKinley's death: "From the first, President McKinley assumed a close personal direction, not only of the organization of the forces but of the general plan of operations. He was Commander-in-Chief not merely in name but in fact." This judgment is correct, as the evidence reveals, but a description of how the president waged his war requires some explanation of the technical methods through which McKinley gathered information and disseminated his decisions.[2]

As the fighting started, the White House staff took over an office on the southeast corner of the second floor, which had previously been used to house executive clerks and leftover correspondence regarding patronage, but it quickly became known as the War Room. Since it adjoined the president's working area, it emerged as the communications nerve center of the government. A switchboard with twenty telegraph wires kept McKinley in touch with French and British cable lines, which ran to Cuba and other points in the Caribbean, as well as American cable lines, which connected him with the soldiers in the field and less directly with the navy. At the height of the fighting in Cuba, messages between the president and General William R. Shafter could be exchanged within twenty minutes. A former executive clerk who was now a lieutenant colonel in the volunteers, Benjamin F. Montgomery, oversaw the cable and telephone traffic inside the War Room and recorded all messages in a running diary of the day's business.

McKinley placed Brigadier General Adolphus W. Greely of the Signal Corps in charge of the government's military communications system. At a cabinet meeting early in the war, the president instructed Greely "to assume charge of all cables, exercise such control over them as is necessary for the public welfare, and is legal."[3] Beginning with only eight hundred dollars and fifty-eight men, the Signal Corps drew on the equipment and personnel of the major telegraph companies to create a network for the army in Cuba. It monitored neutral traffic to determine ship movements, and it had an agent at the telegraph office in Havana whose daily reports revealed, among other things, that the Spanish fleet was at Santiago de Cuba. The corps also found a severed submarine cable off the Cuban coast which became the direct link between American forces and the War Department. By the end of hostilities, Greely and his force, its numbers swelled by volunteers, had become an essential source for the president in making military decisions.

The administration installed in the Executive Mansion fifteen telephone lines that ran directly to the eight executive departments and to the House and Senate. From this "cable box," which had the numbers for each of the departments, the president could now coordinate policies in a manner that previously had not seemed possible. He also employed an early version of the dictaphone, called the graphaphone, to leave messages and instructions for his aides. In the telephone, McKinley found an instrument that fit his liking for a minimum of written actions, and he conducted business over it with increasing frequency after 1898. McKinley's reliance on the telephone and telegraph during the war meant that he "used remote voice communication for the first time to project presidential pres-

Map of the Philippines by Lewis A. Armstrong

The War Room. From the collections of the Library of
Congress

ence into the battle zone on a near real time basis while he remained in Washington."[4]

To follow the progress of the fighting systematically, the War Room received a supply of up-to-date charts and maps of Cuba, the Philippines, and the ocean approaches to the combat zones. The White House staff began to collect this information in April, and the president also drew on the services of the Coast and Geodetic Survey. "It is evident that I must learn a deal of geography in this war," he said to a member of the survey who had brought him maps of the Philippines, "and I am going to turn over to you the task of furnishing me the necessary maps and charts." Soon the maps filled the walls of the War Room, and the clerks recorded the movements of American and Spanish forces. The amount of data at the president's disposal expanded daily as Montgomery, Porter, Cortelyou, and the staff tabulated the locations of enemy, neutral, and United States ships. The War Room sought, and to a large extent achieved, absolute secrecy. To this headquarters, which never closed, McKinley often went in order to monitor events. "By the President's orders, he was to be awakened at any hour of the night if important intelligence should come in." The informational pressures of modern war, because vessels and forces were thousands of miles from Washington, worked with McKinley's fondness for rapid private communication to produce an early crude version of what the twentieth-century presidency would ultimately need in order to meet the demands of world-power diplomacy and the military responsibilities connected with it.[5]

Because the full collection of McKinley's personal papers became available to historians piecemeal and because the president tended to send documents to the department or bureau concerned, an accurate picture of how he shaped strategy as commander in chief can only be assembled from scattered sources. He drafted his directives on the backs of envelopes or on Executive Mansion cards, or he sent them by graphaphone message; so the form of the resulting orders did not always reveal his influence. A mid-June order to General Nelson A. Miles regarding troop dispositions was written in McKinley's own hand, and at a key juncture in negotiations with the Spanish army about its surrender in Cuba, the president inserted tougher language in a telegram to the American commander. Day by day, and sometimes on an hour-to-hour basis, the president oversaw the war. In so doing, he laid the foundation for the modern presidency.

As hostilities began, McKinley made two additional changes in his cabinet. In late 1897 he named Attorney General Joseph McKenna to the Supreme Court. John W. Griggs of New Jersey took his place, soon becoming one of McKinley's closest advisors. Postmaster General James A. Gary stepped down because of ill health, and Charles Emory Smith, owner of the *Philadelphia Press*, succeeded him. The most important shift involved Secretary of State Sherman. For months, McKinley and Day had by-passed Sherman, but the war left no leeway for senility and ineptitude. With growing evidence of Sherman's incapacity, the president secured his resignation on April 25, 1898. Day agreed to serve as secretary of state until the end of the war, and John Bassett Moore, an expert on international law from Columbia University, became first assistant secretary. Moore had advised the state department during Cleveland's second term. Now, as he assumed a large and direct policy-making role, he became an early example of McKinley's policy of enlisting experts and academicians for his government. The Sherman mistake had now been rectified, and McKinley had a functioning team in his most vital executive department. Cabinet changes during McKinley's term worked to improve the quality of his administration. Had he dumped Secretary of War Alger at this point, his government would have been strengthened further. At the outset of the war, however, the impact that such an action would have had on public confidence precluded taking it. McKinley had not yet realized, though he was beginning to see signs, that Alger would fall short as a war leader.

Within two weeks of the start of hostilities the American people learned of Commodore George Dewey's overwhelming triumph against the Spanish at Manila Bay on May 1, 1898. This initial victory in which Dewey sank seven Spanish ships without the loss of any American vessels and with only slight casualties was, according to Senator Cushman K. Davis, "unequalled in the annals of naval warfare."[6] The battle also transformed the war against Spain into a turning point in American history. In the popular mind the immediate thought was not how the United States might avoid decisions over the fate of the Philippines but what the country should do with its prize of war.

In later years, with disillusion about American imperialism in fashion, Dewey's presence at Manila would be attributed to the fortuitous actions of Theodore Roosevelt as assistant secretary of the navy on February 25, 1898. With Secretary of the Navy Long out of the office that day, the impetuous, imperialistic Roosevelt wired Dewey: "In the event of declaration of war Spain, your duty will be to see that the Spanish squadron does not leave the Asiatic coast, and then offensive operations in Philippine Islands." A long-time advocate of a "Large Policy" in Asia, Roosevelt allegedly had seen an opportunity while the McKinley administration was asleep; and acquisition of the Philippines, with all its anguish, was the result. This popular account is dramatic and compelling. McKinley and Long recede into the background, and Roosevelt looms as almost a president three years in advance of becoming one.[7]

The actual sequence of events is more complex, and Roosevelt's message shrinks in importance. Naval planning for an attack on the Philippines dated back to 1895, when the possibility of a Spanish-American conflict over Cuba first arose. A year later the Office of Naval Intelligence proposed, if war came, to strike at Spain at a vulnerable point in its Asian colony. During the next year the Navy first discarded and then readopted this plan as its strategy against Spain. In June 1897 the naval board that was charged with war-planning recommended that an effort should be made to help the rebels against Spanish rule in the islands. A naval assault on Manila might, in aiding the insurgents, obtain for the United States "a controlling voice, as to what should become of the islands, when the final settlement was made."[8] In late October 1897 Commodore Dewey was named commander in chief of the Asiatic Squadron, and the Philippine plan, whose general outlines he already knew, was available to him in early 1898, when he took over his new assignment. As the Cuban crisis worsened, the navy relayed orders to Dewey in accordance with the plan. On January 27 he was told to retain men whose enlistments had expired. Roosevelt's wire of February 25 was part of this preparatory process. It did not change the course of events, nor did Secretary Long, when he returned the next day, rescind it.

The actual directive to attack the Spanish at Manila was based on McKinley's decision. Upon the declaration of war the navy advised Long that "we should strike at once at the Spanish fleet in the Philippines." As Long recalled, the Bureau of Navigation prepared the order, which he approved and McKinley signed. The president postponed action on the order when Long first raised the question on April 21, but three days later, on Sunday, April 24, gave the signal for the attack to begin. Dewey was told to proceed at once to the Philippine Islands. "Commence operations at once, particularly against Spanish fleet. You must capture vessels or destroy. Use utmost endeavor." A week later the battle was over, and Spanish power in the Pacific had been destroyed.[9]

Dewey's victory transformed the military and diplomatic context of the war during its opening week. To the initial aim of ousting Spain from Cuba were now added the alluring possibilities of expanding America's economic and political influence in Asia and the role of being a genuine world power. During the 1890s, interest in the potential markets of China had quickened among some members of the business community. American trade with China, though it did not constitute a large proportion of the nation's total commerce, went up from about $7 million in exports in 1892 to nearly $12 million in 1897. During the first year of McKinley's term, the advocates of a greater trade with China sent in petitions and passed resolutions calling on the administration to protect American interests in Asia. Equally vociferous were the spokesmen for the nation's Protestant churches, who saw the Far East as an arena for an evangelical effort.

The extent to which these pressures actually affected policy-making is debatable. Preoccupied with the Spanish crisis, the McKinley administration had only modest resources with which to carry on an Asian policy before the spring of 1898. It watched the European powers penetrate China in 1897/1898, as France, Russia, Germany, and Great Britain obtained trading privileges or territorial concessions. In December 1897 a cabinet officer told reporters that the government had decided "to keep a watchful eye on the situation as it developed," and the president substituted a veteran diplomat, Edwin H. Conger, for an earlier choice as minister to China. But McKinley did not wish to go beyond diplomatic probing. In March 1898 the British asked whether the United States would join "in opposing any action by foreign Powers which could tend to restrict the opening of China to the commerce of all nations." In the midst of the Cuban problem, the president did no more than assert that he was "in sympathy with the policy which shall maintain open trade" in China.[10]

After Dewey had triumphed over the Spanish, America's displeasure over Spain's rule in Cuba converged with the McKinley administration's desire to broaden the nation's economic role. Somewhere between accident and design, the United States pursued a line of policy that included an opportunistic assault on a vulnerable point for Spain, a generalized awareness that a greater naval presence in the Pacific would support economic initiatives in Asia, and a commitment to the view that foreign markets were a beneficial addition to the nation's search for prosperity. President McKinley never did set down a comprehensive statement of his position on

America's role in the Orient; but he believed, as did many of his countrymen, that good business and proper morality would fuse when western goods and Christian morality penetrated the Far East.

Few historians contend that the president had decided before May 1 to take the Philippines for the United States. Most of them date his decision well before his October 28 message to the peace commissioners in Paris, which instructed them to demand all of the islands from Spain. McKinley's conduct from May 2 onward indicates that he had never given serious consideration to relinquishing the archipelago. The question had always been whether to hold only a portion or to occupy and demand all of it. As a result, he acted in a manner that would ensure the success of any ultimate decision to take the Philippines. Therefore, in the last half of 1898, he exercised the power of his office in a manner that matched many of the assertive actions of his most noteworthy immediate successors, Theodore Roosevelt and Woodrow Wilson.

The administration did not learn officially about Dewey's triumph until May 7, but newspapers on May 2 carried the outlines of what had transpired. As Americans celebrated what seemed to be an outstanding success, the president, Secretaries Long and Alger, and the chief military commanders met at the White House to shape strategy against Spain. It was decided to send five thousand troops to the islands for, in McKinley's words, "such service as may be ordered hereafter." By May 8, as military preparations began, the State Department reported that a member of the British government had asked John Hay, the American ambassador, about terms on which the United States might make peace. As the government explored the origins of this initiative, John Bassett Moore drew up a tentative list of conditions for a settlement. On the Philippines he proposed that Spain retain them, "she ceding to us a coaling station in that group or in the Carolines." Moore noted that the United States did not yet have possession of the islands, and that they might be a bargaining chip in trying to persuade Spain to leave Cuba. The memorandum, which was discussed at a cabinet meeting on May 11, continued to be the basic formulation of the American position into early June.[11]

On the military side, however, the commitment to the Philippines was hardening. By May 11 the number of troops allocated to the expedition had risen to over ten thousand, and the War Department assigned General Wesley Merritt to lead the American forces. The president also arranged to send a geologist to the Philippines to survey their mineral resources, and he began to collect and read the available information on the islands. On May 16 McKinley created the Department of the Pacific, under Merritt's command, a department that was "intended to include Philippine Islands only." His orders to Merritt, which were written on May 19, asserted a "twofold purpose of completing the reduction of the Spanish power in that quarter and of giving order and security to the islands while in the possession of the United States." The president gave the general large powers, under military authority, to set up new legal systems, to raise taxes, and to confiscate property. As to the Philippine rebels, McKinley noted that the American commander, while respecting the existing political arrangements, would be bound "to adopt measures of a different kind if, unfortunately, the course of the people should render such measures indispensable to the maintenance of law and order." On May 29 the size of Merritt's force was again increased, to twenty thousand men. It was evident, said a Washington reporter in early June, that "the United States has no idea of surrendering the newly acquired territory in the Far East."[12]

The president also threw his influence behind the renewed effort on Capitol Hill to secure the annexation of Hawaii by joint resolution. Ambassador Hay wired the State Department on May 3 that "an excellent authority in German matters" recommended "prompt action in annexation Hawaii before war closes as otherwise Germany might seek to complicate the question with Samoa or Philippine Islands." The islands would be vital if the United States had to carry on a campaign in the Philippines; there the soldiers and sailors could obtain food, water, and exercise, while their ships were refueling from Hawaiian coal supplies. On May 4 a Democratic congressman, Francis G. Newlands of Nevada, introduced a resolution in the House, and Secretary Day helped to obtain favorable action on the resolution in the House Foreign Affairs Committee on May 12. Reported to the full House on May 17, the Hawaiian measure encountered the determined opposition of Speaker Reed. For three weeks the Speaker, a bitter enemy of McKinley's who opposed expansionism on principle, blocked consideration of the resolution. The White House issued material to the press, questioning whether Reed could persist indefinitely in tactics "which may excite the active and open antagonism of a large majority of his party in the House." McKinley called congressmen to his office to emphasize the utmost importance of annexation. News leaks raised the prospect that the president would simply seize Hawaii under the war power. By early June, Reed had yielded to presidential pressure. Floor debate began on June 11, and the resolution passed four days later by 209 to 91.[13]

The resolution reached the Senate on June 17, coming up for debate on June 20; and the discussion went on until July 6. The opposition was composed primarily of Democrats, though some Republicans, wary of expansion, resisted as well. When the anti-annexation forces pressed for an early adjournment in order to forestall a vote, McKinley said, in the press and privately, that "there must be no thought of adjournment until Hawaii was acted upon."[14] Presidential lobbying succeeded when the Senate voted 42 in favor, 21 against, and 26 not voting, for the resolution on July 6. The outbreak of the Spanish-American War did not turn Hawaiian annexation from a failure into a triumph in Congress. The war did not transform the balance of voting power in the Senate. The annexationists had about 55 votes in their column in January, and allocation of the 26 nonvoters in July indicates that they were still several votes short of the required two-thirds. The basic strategy for securing annexation by joint resolution was developed before the Cuban crisis had intensified, and McKinley's pressure was a central element in the ultimate victory. The annexation of Hawaii belongs among the legislative accomplishments of his first term.

On the question of the Philippines the administration kept to the position that it had adopted in early May through the first week of June. When Ambassador Hay again reported a strong desire in London about terms of a possible peace, Secretary Day and Moore reviewed the May 9 memorandum with the president. On June 3 Hay was told that "the President, speaking for himself, would be inclined to grant terms of peace" on the basis of Spanish evacuation of Cuba, the cession of Puerto Rico to the United States, and the granting of an island, probably Guam, in the Ladrones in the Pacific. The Philippines would "be allowed to remain with Spain, except a port and necessary appurtenances, to be selected by the United States, shall be ceded to the United States." At the same time, the military commitment swelled as more ships and additional troops moved to embarkation points in San Francisco.[15]

By the middle of June, however, McKinley and his advisors were compelled to recognize an additional element in the Philippine situation. In 1896 Emilio Aguinaldo led an insurrection against Spanish rule in the islands. After a year of fighting, the rebels concluded an agreement with Spain in December 1897 that called for the voluntary exile of the leaders of the revolt, cash payments from Spain, and an amnesty. During the next three months the revolutionaries regrouped, and fighting resumed in March 1898. After the war with Spain had commenced, the American consul in Singapore, E. Spencer Pratt, met with Aguinaldo on April 24; then Pratt reported to Dewey at Hong Kong that the rebel commander would arrange for "general cooperation [with the] insurgents [in] Manila if desired." Dewey wired back that Aguinaldo should come as soon as possible; but before the Filipino could reach Hong Kong, the United States Fleet had left for Manila. Two weeks later, Dewey permitted Aguinaldo to come on an American vessel to Manila, where he "was received with great enthusiasm by the natives."[16]

Once he had returned, Aguinaldo continued to organize his revolution. He issued a proclamation on May 24, saying that the United States had come "manifesting a protection as decisive as it is undoubtedly disinterested toward our inhabitants, considering us as sufficiently civilized and capable of governing for ourselves our unfortunate country." He set up a "dictatorial government," and he also published decrees regulating the revolt against the Spanish. The administration reacted quickly to Aguinaldo's presence. A dispatch from Dewey, reporting that the Filipino leader was "organizing forces near Cavite and may render assistance that will be valuable," reached Washington on May 25. It was given to McKinley, and he replied, through Long: "It is desirable, as far as possible, and consistent for your success and safety, not to have political alliances with the insurgents or any faction in the islands that would incur our liability to maintain their cause in the future." Two weeks later the State Department received reports from the consuls in Singapore and Manila that discussed their cooperation in arranging for Aguinaldo's journey to the Philippines, cooperation that in Pratt's words had "prevented possible conflict of action and facilitated the work of occupying and administering the Philippines."[17]

Combined with other information about insurgent activity, however, these messages prompted the McKinley administration to reconsider its posture toward the islands. Hay was informed on June 14 that conditions in the June 3 peace terms would "probably have to be modified. The insurgents there have become an important factor in the situation and must have just consideration in any terms of settlement." Dewey was ordered the same day to report fully on any previous conferences with Aguinaldo and to inform Washington of any additional meetings.[18]

The State Department, conveying "the President's views on the subject of your relations with General Aguinaldo," instructed Consul Pratt, on June 16, to "avoid unauthorized negotiations with Philippine insurgents." In a fuller statement, Secretary Day warned that "this Government has known the Philippine insurgents only as discontented and rebellious subjects of Spain, and is not acquainted with their purposes." Any action taken by Pratt that involved cooperation with Aguinaldo's plans or that recognized "any political claims which he may put forward" was unauthorized and disapproved.[19]

While preventing any formal political contacts with the insurgents, McKinley told callers that though he was undecided about the eventual status of the Philippines, he favored "the general principle of holding on to what we get." As he noted in a personal memorandum at the start of the war: "While we are conducting war and until its conclusion we must keep all we get; when the war is over we must keep what we want." To Henry Cabot Lodge and others, McKinley expressed the hope that the "insurgents will develop enough strength to solve the problem by setting up a government of their own under our protection—we to keep Manila," and he worried about "the questions of race, climate, etc.," that made him "doubtful . . . about our keeping the whole group." But he added significantly, "If, however as we go on it is made to appear desirable that we should retain all, then we will certainly do it."[20]

Whatever the president had decided at this point, and his qualms are less telling than his actions, he was careful to keep his options open and his purposes obscure. By the time that American troops reached the Philippines on June 30, the direction of McKinley's policy was clear to informed observers in Washington. In carrying on negotiations over peace, said a cabinet member to the press, the United States would insist that Spain relinquish its sovereignty over Cuba, Puerto Rico, and the Philippines. Such negotiations, however, depended on the outcome of fighting in Cuba; and at the end of June, American and Spanish forces faced each other outside Santiago de Cuba.

Before the war with Spain had begun, advocates of a belligerent policy had predicted that if fighting should come, the conquest of Cuba would be easy. These optimistic forecasts had faded when United States troops went ashore near Santiago de Cuba in late June. President McKinley found that even a small war in the late nineteenth century required greater societal exertions than had been anticipated. Therefore the White House spent the first two months of the conflict raising an army, devising a strategy, and responding to the naval actions of the enemy. While these activities were occurring, the public passed from initial enthusiasm to impatience for action to a skepticism about the performance of the army and the War Department that persisted long after the hostilities had ended.

As his fostering of a modern communications capacity revealed, William McKinley expected to play the decisive part in the management of the war effort. He soon decided that the civilian and military subordinates at his disposal were not adequate to their responsibilities, and he moved to limit their influence on his policies. Secretary of War Alger, who had only recently recuperated from a heart-connected illness, displayed an inordinate sense of egotism, which impaired the efficiency of his department. His information was not always reliable, especially his optimistic predictions in April and May about how quickly the volunteer soldiers would be ready for duty. He interfered in details of mobilization, quarreled with senior army officers, and seemed to the president to make promises and then to equivocate about the War Department's performance. McKinley was already disillusioned with Alger by the late spring; the public outcry over disease in the army camps and in Cuba, as well as the state of the food that the troops received, would in the summer combine to make Alger a positive liability.

The commanding general of the army, Nelson A. Miles, who was nationally prominent, was a striking physical embodiment of the military presence. He was also vain and impractical in the high councils of the government and had presidential ambitions. McKinley wearied of his posturing, but could have forgiven that had the general not blundered over the selection of rifles for the army, erred in the choice of campsites for the volunteers, and feuded with Alger over minor points of procedure.

Looking elsewhere for reliable counsel, McKinley first turned to General James M. Schofield. The former commanding general proved to be only a modest improvement on Miles. As his advice produced disruption and rancor, Schofield gave way to the adjutant general, Henry C. Corbin. A friend of many leaders among Ohio Republicans, Corbin was smooth where Miles grated and was efficient where Alger was not. By May 1898 Corbin had McKinley's confidence and soon emerged as the most influential officer in Washington. "In all the work of organizing, planning, and operating," Charles Emory Smith remembered, "the President relied on his judgment and execution."[21] He was, in effect, the commander of the army, and he retained McKinley's trust until September 1901. With Alger's cooperation, Corbin enabled the War Department to function with greater effectiveness. In particular, he encouraged individual initiative among commanders in the Quartermaster and Medical bureaus and fostered the same spirit in line officers.

The army that McKinley and Corbin directed had changed rapidly from the 25,000 regular officers and men who were in uniform at the beginning of 1898. The War Department, when faced with the likelihood of a conflict, had originally planned to expand the army from the existing base of regular troops to a force of approximately 75,000 to 100,000 men. These soldiers, army planners thought, would be enough to meet any challenge that Spain posed, after the navy had defeated the enemy fleet. Expansion required congressional action, and a bill, sponsored by Congressman John A. T. Hull of Iowa, was introduced on March 17. During a war, the bill said, the president could raise the army's authorized strength to 104,000 men. Building upon the existing structure of regiments and companies, the bill envisioned a minimal part for volunteers and the National Guard. At the end of March the Hull bill seemed to be assured of prompt approval.

Patriotic fervor and the opposition of the National Guard soon caused the Hull measure to stall. Volunteers disapproved of the prospect of serving under regular officers, and the National Guard would have been all but excluded under the proposed legislation. When the Hull bill was debated on April 6 in the House, it encountered withering criticism from a coalition of National Guard supporters, Southern Democrats, and Populists. Even when the sponsors of the bill made substantial concessions to its opponents, the House returned it to committee on April 7 by a sizeable vote. With war only weeks away, the War Department's mobilization program was in ruins.

As the administration reshaped its thinking about the expansion of the army, it took into account the power of congressional sentiment in favor of a volunteer force. Discussions with National Guard leaders in mid April resulted in plans to have the president raise a force of volunteers who would come from the states and could serve in their National Guard units when they enlisted as a body. Once in the service, the organization of these units would have to correspond to that of the regulars. An initial call for 60,000 troops was contemplated, and the president would be responsible for appointing all volunteer officers. A bill embodying these provisions cleared Congress on April 22, but a call for 60,000 men would not have allowed all the prospective National Guard volunteers to enlist. With the Hull bill, which the army wanted, hung up in the House, the administration expanded the call for volunteers to 125,000 men.

On April 23 McKinley issued his first summons for volunteers in that amount, and the National Guard was appeased. The Hull legislation, which enlarged the regular army to 61,000 men, passed both houses easily and became law on April 26, 1898.

As a result of the popular eagerness to join the army, said Francis E. Warren, the War Department building was "filled daily so that both sides nearly bulge out with a steaming, surging and sometimes nasty crowd who are insisting for places." Secretary Alger saw an average of one hundred visitors a day about appointments, and a comparable number descended on McKinley. In May, Cortelyou attributed the strain on the president in part to "the struggle for place among the ambitious gentlemen who desire to serve their country in high salaried and high titled positions."[22]

The president devoted a large amount of time to these personnel decisions because of their obvious political implications and because of his desire to make the war an occasion to enhance national unity. The appointments of Fitzhugh Lee of Virginia and Joseph Wheeler of Alabama as major generals, along with the selection of other southerners and Democrats for lesser commissions, conciliated the South. While he gave numerous staff positions to relatives of prominent Republicans, McKinley did not neglect Democrats, nor did he put professional competence aside when he chose regular or volunteer officers.

At the outbreak of the war the American people apparently expected that the performance of the armed services would demonstrate the nation's material and military superiority. The highly professional and efficient navy lived up to these assumptions with Dewey's victory at Manila Bay and the later triumph at Santiago. By allowing his officers to execute their duties with only a minimum of direction, Secretary Long impressed McKinley as being a reliable cabinet officer whose actions contributed to the war effort and benefited the administration. The War Department was much less successful. The difficulties that it encountered and the blunders that it made soon aroused a popular distrust of Secretary Alger. The chorus of attacks on the record of the secretary and the department grew so loud in early June that Alger told reporters: "When war was declared, we were unprepared, yet obstacles almost insurmountable have been overcome." Alger would issue more defenses of his record, but cries for his resignation dotted the nation's editorial pages.[23]

In the spring of 1898 the War Department confronted conditions that would have hampered the most vigorous and effective administrator. Years of congressional penny-pinching, in response to the society's neglect of the army, had left only the nucleus of a modern armed service. In its internal organization the department lacked central authority; power was diffused among civilian officials, generals, and competing bureaus. The prospect of war with Spain had not produced much specific preparedness activity before mid April. The bulk of the money for national defense that Congress allocated in March went to the navy. With war unlikely in the 1890s, no comprehensive plan existed for equipping and training a large army of volunteers. American policy makers assumed that the navy would defeat the Spanish at sea and that an expanded regular force would prosecute a campaign in Cuba. The outcome of the Hull bill in Congress put those expectations aside, and the army turned to raising, training, and outfitting the 278,000 men who saw active service.

The first month of the war exposed all the weaknesses that neglect and parsimony had inflicted upon the army. Of the five thousand wagons needed to move men and supplies, there were only twelve hundred on hand. Delays in production were not overcome until after the war. Ammunition supplies were also inadequate. Had all the soldiers who had been mobilized seen combat, there would not have been enough bullets for them. The modern Krag-Jorgensen rifle could only be given to regular troops because there were shortages of the weapon and of the smokeless powder that it used. Uniforms, tents, cartridge belts, and mess kits were not available in the needed amounts, and supply officers improvised in order to meet the requirements of the burgeoning number of troops. The supply of food was, from the first, generally sufficient; but experiments with canned roast beef led to a postwar controversy over the army's meat supply.

Conditions in the camps where the troops assembled offered the most public evidence of the problems that the War Department faced. The army's outmoded and inefficient procedures could not deal with the masses of men to be fed, housed, clothed, and trained in the early weeks of the war. Few officers knew how to manage large numbers of troops, and conflicting responsibilities among quartermaster, ordnance, and medical officers caused frictions that multiplied the disorganization. Some camps had too much of a particular piece of equipment; others were short of everything. The most notorious camp was the one at Tampa, Florida, where a single rail line served a force of seventeen thousand men.

Some of the trouble lay with the lack of preparedness of the

National Guard. Many members were reluctant to volunteer for two years, and the units that entered the service were not as well trained as their advocates had predicted. Fewer states than anticipated were able to equip their soldiers to the standards of the army. The War Department struggled, with increasing success, to surmount these obstacles by June 1898. Alger and Corbin granted authority to officers on the scene, and as these men began to deal with immediate problems, a greater sense of order and direction emerged. By the end of July the army was in a condition of readiness and efficiency that surpassed what might have been hoped for in the near-chaos of May. Unfortunately for Alger and the McKinley administration, the first impression of bungling and confusion continued to be the fixed public memory of the army's performance. The course of the war and its consequences for American troops in Cuba only confirmed the initial verdict about Alger's ineptitude and the army's shortcomings.

Developments that had the greatest influence on the performance of the army and the War Department, causing them to make changes in strategy, were Spanish naval actions, shifts in American foreign policy, and the hazards of a land campaign in Cuba. After the fighting had ended, McKinley pondered over how the fortunes of war had affected the president's conduct as commander in chief. In Boston in February 1899 he said: "The President can direct the movement of soldiers in the field and fleets upon the sea, but he cannot foresee the close of such movements or prescribe their limits. He cannot anticipate or avoid the consequences, but he must meet them."[24] McKinley was recalling how his own priorities and war aims had adjusted to alterations in the military and diplomatic situation that confronted the United States.

In mid April the administration expected the main combat activity to be naval. Once the American fleet had defeated its Spanish counterpart, an invasion of Cuba would be considered. Because the army was unprepared and because there was a real danger of malaria and yellow fever on the island during the summer months, it seemed more prudent to rely on a naval blockade, to launch some armed raids against the Spanish forces, and to furnish arms and material to the rebels. Spanish troops in Cuba numbered about eighty thousand effective fighting men, and the capture of Havana would be a task of some difficulty. On April 20 a conference at the White House ratified these decisions. The navy blockaded Cuba on April 23, and the army prepared to send an expedition of five thousand men to the southern coast of Cuba to link up with the rebels under Máximo Gómez and to supply them with arms. A representative of the Cuban junta wrote to McKinley on April 26 to promise "the most complete co-operation of the Cuban army with the military forces of the United States." He added that "to save the lives of the unacclimated American troops," the Cubans were ready, "if arms and ammunition are promptly provided, to stand the brunt of the fighting on the Island."[25] On April 29 General William R. Shafter was directed to conduct a strike in Cuba, among other things, to help the insurgents.

The Spanish Fleet, under Admiral Pascual de Cervera, left the Cape Verde islands in the Atlantic that same day, "and for almost two weeks the Navy Department floundered in a sea of ignorance as to his whereabouts." The effective disappearance of the Spanish ships, a detachment whose fighting capacity was not underestimated, caused the Shafter expedition to be postponed on April 30. Troops continued to flow to the American base at Tampa during May. Though the port and its nearby town were adequate for the assembling of the rather small raiding force that had originally been envisioned, they were ill suited for a much larger number of troops. By the end of the month, seventeen thousand men were crowded into the camp. Two weeks later, Theodore Roosevelt, now an officer with the First Volunteer Cavalry, told his friend Henry Cabot Lodge that "no words could describe to you the confusion and lack of system and the general mismanagement of affairs here." As General Shafter explained to his superiors: "The place was over-estimated and its capacities are exceeded."[26]

The expansion of the force at Tampa also reflected changes in the administration's strategy toward Cuba. The defeat of the Spanish Fleet at Manila reduced the fears about Cervera's potential effectiveness in the Caribbean; therefore the Atlantic Fleet did not appear in Cuban waters in early May, when the sailing time that had been projected for Cervera should have brought him there. Adding to the pressure for an invasion of the island were the navy's problems in sustaining a blockade of the Cuban coast and the more optimistic evaluations of the dangers from disease in Cuba. If the United States remained passive, moreover, the chances of European intervention might reappear. Finally, political control of the island's destiny at the end of the fighting could hinge on the ability of the United States to dominate the rebels with troops on the ground.

At the May 2 conference, where the Philippines expedition was arranged, McKinley decided to authorize an invasion of Cuba, with Havana as the primary target. Fifty thousand troops would compose the main force, and Alger said that they would be ready in less than three weeks. The president and the secretary of war expected that volunteers would supplement the regulars to make up the invading army. During that same week, Shafter told Washington that his troops could commence the campaign after May 12. In response he was ordered on May 9 to seize a position on Cuba's north coast from which an army could operate. A series of delays and obstacles now upset this timetable. First, the navy sought a postponement until May 16, so that it could assemble its ships to escort Shafter's soldiers. Attempts to coordinate the movement of volunteers revealed that they were less prepared than the administration had anticipated. Shortages of ammunition and deficiencies of fresh water at Key West prompted General Miles to urge McKinley to postpone the invasion in favor of an attack on Puerto Rico. Then, on May 13, Admiral Cervera's fleet was sighted off Martinique. The presence of the enemy caused the War Department to put off the attack on Havana, which nevertheless continued to be the primary target through the end of May.

A week later, on May 19, Greely's telegraph service reported that, according to a spy in Havana, Cervera's forces had escaped the American ships that were looking for him and had slipped into the harbor of Santiago de Cuba, on the southern side of the island. By May 29 the navy had confirmed that Cervera was at Santiago, and on June 1 the bulk of the American fleet, under Admiral William T. Sampson, bottled up the Spanish. Acting on the news from Greely, McKinley assembled another war council on May 26, 1898, which consisted of Alger, Long, Miles, and three navy representatives, including Captain Alfred T. Mahan. Miles argued that the assault on Havana should be shelved in favor of an expedition against Santiago and an attack on Puerto Rico. McKinley agreed. Santiago was appealing as an objective because it offered an isolated force of ten thousand Spaniards and the opportunity to destroy a substantial portion of the enemy's naval strength; its seizure would also aid in capturing Puerto Rico. Miles's idea contained some grandiose aspects, including a cavalry thrust across central Cuba. McKinley disapproved of these. On May 31 Corbin instructed Shafter to land near Santiago de Cuba and to "capture or destroy the garrison there" while aiding the navy to deal with the Spanish Fleet. Conveying McKinley's wishes, Corbin reminded the American commander of "the importance of accomplishing this object with the least possible delay." Meanwhile, Puerto Rico would be attacked, once Santiago had fallen.[27]

It required almost two weeks to load Shafter's troops for the voyage to Cuba. Tampa was by this time a tangled confusion of men, supplies, and animals. McKinley sent peremptory telegrams through Alger and Corbin, asking Shafter: "When you will get away?" The general answered that "it seems we are awfully slow in getting off, but I have been working night and day since I have been here." The president's patience with the delay in sailing wore away until, on the evening of June 7, with the loading process already begun, he ordered Shafter "to sail at once with what force you have ready." By the next day, after a disorganized scramble to get on board the ships, the American flotilla was on its way. An erroneous report that Spanish ships had been sighted then caused a postponement of the sailing until June 14. The expedition, as Theodore Roosevelt wrote, was "packed and sweltering on these troop ships in Tampa Bay under the semi-tropical June sun."[28] Finally the invasion force left Florida, arriving off Santiago on June 20. Following consultations with Admiral Sampson and General Calixto Garcia of the Cuban rebels, Shafter sent his soldiers onto the island on June 22. Four days later the landings were completed.

General William R. Shafter was a veteran of the Civil War, where he won the Medal of Honor, and he had fought Indians in the Southwest during the late 1860s and 1870s. But he lacked experience in handling large military formations, and he was not a good administrator in the field. Worst of all, he did not look like a general. At sixty-three years of age, he was fat and slovenly. But these weaknesses and his weight were balanced by his good sense, his determination, and his ability to make a decision. His appointment owed little to the Michigan background and veterans' work that he shared with Alger. Generals Corbin and Miles both recommended him to McKinley, and the president accepted the judgment of his highest military advisors.

With the war now in its land-combat phase, President McKinley followed Shafter's progress, as well as the naval engagement that accompanied it, by means of the telegraph in the War Room. On June 24, American soldiers, including the Rough Riders, had a sharp fight with the Spaniards at Las Guasimas, and Shafter sent his troops against the Spanish fortifications outside Santiago on July 1. The day-long battle for San Juan Hill ended with the Americans being in possession of the first line of the city's defenses. The cost in dead and wounded had been heavy.

Despite the direct contact with Shafter's headquarters, the

White House could only wait through the long hours of July 1 for word on the progress of the battle. The general had said that he would keep the War Department continually advised, but it was late evening before he reported that his army was in possession of the "outer works" of the Spanish. The first casualty reports were "above 400," but then Shafter's second message said that he had underestimated them. The telegraph then fell silent until July 3, when he informed Washington that he could not assault Santiago successfully, had suffered heavy losses, and was "seriously considering withdrawing about 5 miles" to new positions. He did not reveal that he had also asked the Spanish commander in Santiago to surrender. Secretary Alger replied: "Of course you can judge the situation better than we can at this end of the line"; but in words that had probably been cleared with McKinley, Alger added: "If, however, you could hold your present position, especially San Juan heights, the effect upon the country would be much better than falling back." Shafter had noted that his own health was not good, and Corbin wired him that afternoon: "The Secretary of War, no less than the President, is very desirous to know how you are feeling to-day."[29]

If the president's inquiry displayed a certain impatience, McKinley's apprehensive state of mind on July 3 is understandable. Reports reaching Washington indicated that Cervera's fleet had broken out of Santiago Harbor and escaped. A further dispatch that evening left the outcome of the naval battle in doubt, though a subsequent message from Greely's Signal Corps confirmed a complete American triumph. On the Fourth of July a telegram came from Admiral Sampson announcing that Cervera's fleet had been destroyed. The nation broke into celebrations as the full magnitude of the victory emerged. In a running fight the Americans had destroyed all the decrepit enemy vessels. General Shafter added to the pleasure in the White House late on July 3, first with the news that he had demanded the surrender of the Spanish in the city and later with the pledge that he would hold his position. Spain's position was manifestly hopeless, but the president faced more than a month of decisions and diplomacy before the fighting officially ended.

Negotiations between Shafter and the Spanish general in Santiago, José Toral, consumed the two weeks after the assault on San Juan Hill and the naval battle. McKinley closely monitored Shafter's discussions, and he kept his commander tied to the president's purposes. On July 8 Toral proposed to evacuate the city if his

Early morning advance to San Juan. Photography Collection, Humanities Research Center, University of Texas at Austin

U.S. troops at Bloody Bend. Photography Collection, Humanities Research Center, University of Texas at Austin

Theodore Roosevelt and the Rough Riders on San Juan Hill. Theodore Roosevelt Collection, Harvard College Library, Cambridge, Massachusetts

troops would be allowed to retreat to another location with their equipment and weapons. Shafter advised Washington to accept, because this would free Santiago Harbor, save civilian and military lives, and relieve his forces, among whom three cases of yellow fever had been found. McKinley had become dubious about the general's fighting ability. After consulting with Alger and Corbin on July 4, he authorized a message to be sent to Shafter, expressing "sorrow and anxiety" about his illness and telling him that he "must determine whether your condition is such as to require you to relinquish command." Shafter said no more about his health, and he accepted the presence of General Miles, who was sent from Washington to aid him. When Shafter's telegram about the Spanish truce proposal came in, McKinley dealt with it personally.[30]

The government's response went out over Corbin's signature in the third person. A draft containing the president's corrections survives. Shafter was reminded that he had said early in the day that his position was impregnable and that the Spanish "would yet surrender unconditionally" because the Americans could cut off their supplies. "Under these circumstances," the president continued, "your message recommending that Spanish troops be permitted to evacuate and proceed without molestation to Holguin is a great surprise and is not approved." Another presidential telegram followed: "What you went to Santiago for was the Spanish army. If you allow it to evacuate with its arms you must meet it somewhere else. This is not war."[31]

While he peremptorily rejected the idea of allowing the Spanish to evacuate, McKinley was more receptive to Alger's proposal that the United States transport the enemy troops who were in Santiago back to Spain once they had surrendered. This offer was made to Toral on July 10, but he said no. On July 10 and 11 the Americans and the Spanish fought a rifle and artillery duel at long range. When truce negotiations resumed on July 12, Toral once again asked to be allowed to leave the city under honorable conditions. The president was still adamant against any change in the instructions of July 9. At this juncture, Generals Shafter and Miles introduced a new element into the military calculations. Following an exposition of why a truce would be advisable, Miles said, in a message sent early on July 13: "There are 100 cases of yellow fever in this command and the opinion of the surgeon [is] that it will spread rapidly."[32]

The president called a cabinet meeting that day, which turned into "a long sit-down of two or three hours." Secretary Long wrote that the administration was "pained at the delays at Santiago" and that it was "inclined to think" that the American officers who were negotiating with the Spanish were being deceived "with truces and offers of terms of surrender." There was some bickering between Secretary Alger and Captain Mahan, who was a member of the naval war board and directed that service's strategy, over army-navy cooperation or lack of it in breaking the siege. Then the president decided to press Toral to surrender in accordance with the terms that had already been proposed. Miles and Shafter were told to attack, "unless in your judgment an assault would fail." As to the yellow-fever problem, troops were to be sent, once the Spanish had given up, to camps "on high ground near the coast and within easy reach of their base of supplies." Other measures were ordered for the purpose of minimizing the possible spread of the disease.[33]

While the cabinet was deliberating, Miles and Shafter conferred again with Toral, giving him twenty-four hours in which to capitulate or face another attack. Hearing of this, Alger renewed the offer to send the Spanish prisoners across the Atlantic. Faced with the prospect of a naval bombardment and an attack from Shafter's men, Toral asked for and received from his superior in Havana the permission to surrender. When the peace talks resumed, the scheduled American attacks were called off. Two days of negotiation brought about a Spanish capitulation on July 17. Toral's officers kept their sidearms, and the United States agreed to transport their enemies home. In return, Shafter obtained the surrender of Santiago and the rest of eastern Cuba.

As the surrender of Santiago neared, General Miles moved on to attack Puerto Rico. His troops, which landed on July 25, conquered most of the island, except for San Juan, with only slight losses during the two weeks that remained of the war. In contrast to the confusion in Cuba, the supply problems in the Puerto Rican campaign were minimal. Few newspapermen accompanied Miles, and the efficiency and speed of this army exercise did not receive the publicity that attended the events in Cuba.

By the last weeks in June, with American troops in Cuba, sentiment in Spain for a negotiated peace gathered strength. The main source of opposition to a peace initiative was the army. One reason for the suicidal effort of the Spanish Fleet to escape from Santiago was to demonstrate that every means of military resistance had been tried. The destruction of Cervera's vessels made the reinforcement and resupply of the army impossible. With their navy destroyed, the Spanish could not support their forces in the colonies, and the coast of the homeland lay exposed to the American navy. The foreign minister said to the French ambassador on July 9: "Our troops are ready to continue the struggle." Nine days later, after Santiago had fallen and American troops were advancing in Puerto Rico and building their numbers in the Philippines, Spain asked France to approach the United States about "negotiation of a suspension of hostilities, preliminary to definitive peace negotiations." On July 22 Jules Cambon, the French ambassador to the United States, was directed to represent Spain in peace discussions. After delays over decoding and transmitting the Spanish message to Cambon, he went to the White House on July 26, a few minutes after three o'clock in the afternoon.[34]

From the outset of the war, President McKinley had been willing to begin peace talks. He told John Bassett Moore that he wanted "not only to bring the war to a speedy conclusion, but so to conduct it as to leave no lasting animosities behind to prejudice the future friendship and commerce of the two countries." A statement of American terms, however, required that there first be an overture from Madrid. In his proclamation of thanksgiving for the naval victory at Santiago, McKinley's reference to a "just and honorable peace" seemed to diplomats in Washington to be a signal that, as Ambassador Pauncefote said, "these people want peace ardently, but they don't want a middleman." Spain would have to act. By mid July, peace talk was in the air in Europe and in Washington. These negotiations involved a continuing test of McKinley's diplomatic resolve; they also opened up the question of the Philippines to some definite statement of the intentions of the United States.[35]

During the hour that Ambassador Cambon spent with McKinley and Day, he endeavored first to limit the peace parleys to the issue of Cuba. If the fate of the island could be decided, he went on, there would cease to be any reason for continuing the war. Day immediately answered that he understood Cambon to say that "Spain, while she limits herself to asking that we seek by common agreement a solution to the Cuban question, wants to know under what conditions it would be possible to terminate hostilities in all points where they now exist." After Cambon's equivocal answer, McKinley inquired if Cambon had received any proposals from Spain, and a subsequent meeting was arranged, when the French diplomat would bring back Spain's response. The peace talks would, however, deal with Puerto Rico and the Philippines as well as Cuba. That afternoon the waiting reporters were told that Cambon had brought "a message from the Spanish Government looking

to the termination of the war and the settlement of terms of peace."
The Spanish overtures were, said James Wilson privately, "round-
about, indefinite, and all that." Nonetheless, they required that the
president and his advisors hammer out an American position on the
Philippines.[36]

Several days of cabinet meetings, at least one of which was on
a presidental boat on the Potomac, followed Cambon's July 26
interview. The administration had not only to consider the new
diplomatic and military situation that the war had produced but
also to decide the fate of the Philippines in light of the ambitions
of other world powers and the goals of the insurgents on the ground.
The overall military balance clearly favored the United States. Yet
Spain's bargaining position had certain advantages that could, in
the absence of a firm American stand, shift the scales away from
McKinley.

The emergence of the United States as a force in world affairs
had reshaped the nation's relationship to several of the European
powers. In the case of Great Britain, the war had accelerated the
improvement in the friendship between the one-time adversaries
that McKinley had begun. In Britain the American flag flew prom-
inently, the Fourth of July was celebrated, and politicians spoke
fervently of Anglo-Saxon unity. The British government, seeing the
United States as a counterweight to Germany's ambitions, interposed no objections to American expansion and even prepared to
negotiate a resolution of the questions concerning Alaska's boundary and the isthmian canal. As to the fate of the Philippines,
London not only wanted Washington to hold the islands but also
made it clear that the British would want a voice in the disposition
of the archipelago if the Americans were to withdraw.

Among the other European powers, Germany seemed to represent the greatest obstacle to American action in the Pacific. Though
Berlin had revealed from the beginning of the war that it would not
challenge the United States in the Philippines, the Germans had also
emphasized that they would not be so accommodating to an independent republic in the islands. On June 2 the German Navy
ordered Admiral Otto von Diedrichs to Manila with the Asiatic
squadron to join other European vessels that were observing American naval tactics. By the middle of July the American ambassador
in Berlin was reporting that the Germans had designs on the islands,
should the Americans leave. As Hay told Day after conversing with
the German ambassador to Great Britain, Berlin wanted a "few
coaling stations" out of "the final disposition of the Philippines."[37]

Amid the excitement of the news of the Santiago victory on July 4, a telegram from Dewey in Manila mentioned possible interference by the Germans. The admiral's relations with the German squadron had been difficult in June and July, but they were nothing like the melodrama that subsequent legends ascribed to his dealings with von Diedrichs. No British ships, for example, ever interposed themselves between the American vessels, which were attacking Manila, and the German ships, which might otherwise have been tempted to interfere. Two days after Dewey's wire, on July 6, he and the Germans disagreed sharply over whether they could identify neutral ships through the process of visit and search. By July 14 the tensions in the islands had eased. On July 13, however, Dewey informed Washington that the Germans had interfered with the Philippine insurgents. Simultaneously, Ambassador Andrew D. White was learning from the German Foreign Office that Berlin wanted "one or two positions in the Philippines group." Suggesting that Anglo-American cooperation might provoke a Continental coalition against the United States, he hoped that favorable assurances could be given with regard to what Berlin wanted. McKinley responded, through Day, that there was no need for Germany to be apprehensive about British-American relations, that the United States did not possess the Philippines, and that it could "deal with the matters suggested in your cipher telegram and with the whole situation in the end much better and upon broader terms if not pressed for assurances for which no occasion has arisen." At the time of Cambon's appearance with the Spanish proposal, the administration was alert to the prospect that abandonment of the Philippines would mean a more substantial German presence, and probably an eventual foothold, if not outright dominance.[38]

Equally troubling to those who were making calculations about the Philippines were the intentions of the insurgents. The first detachment of the army, some twenty-five hundred men, arrived on June 30 at Manila, and the second contingent, numbering thirty-five hundred, landed on July 17. At the end of the month a third group, of forty-eight hundred, reached Manila. The army officers under General Merritt did not meet or confer with the Filipino leader, who had about twelve thousand soldiers besieging Manila in a desultory campaign. The insurgents had proclaimed their independence on June 12, and Aguinaldo had asked McKinley to leave the Philippines "free and independent, even if you make peace with Spain." From Dewey the administration learned in late June that "the United States has not been bound in any way to assist insurgents by any act or promises, and he is not, to my knowledge, committed to assist us."[39]

John Bassett Moore submitted a memorandum entitled "Relations of the U.S. to Philippine Insurgents" to the president and Secretary Day on July 20. In it he reviewed the consular dispatches of April to June and then concluded that "no authorized act would therefore appear to have been done that can rightly embarrass the action of the Government." If the United States should decide against the insurgents, the memorandum contended, Aguinaldo and his allies would "accuse the United States of improper treatment of them, but without good ground." The possibility that the Filipinos would resist American domination appears to have received little attention.[40]

American public opinion, in the forms that reached President McKinley, seemed to give solid support to an expansionist policy in the Philippines. Grover Cleveland came out against "the seductive words of conquest and expansion" in June 1898, and William Jennings Bryan, shortly before he entered the army as a colonel in the Nebraska Volunteers, expressed to his Democratic brethren similar sentiments against taking the islands. Editorial opinion, however, was recorded as being strongly in favor of expansion, with about 40 percent of the papers that were surveyed being for it and 25 percent against. Political attitudes within the Republican party, which were no doubt shaped by McKinley's actions, endorsed taking the archipelago. The United States had a mission "clearly appointed by Divine Providence" in the Philippines, wrote Senator Joseph B. Foraker, and the nation would fail "to fully manifest its purposes if we allow the Philippines to remain under the yoke and in the midnight darkness to which they have been subjected." Others spoke of markets and how the new possessions could be "pickets of the Pacific, standing guard at the entrances to trade with the millions of China and Korea, French Indo-China, the Malay Peninsula, and the islands of Indonesia." Partisan reasons also entered the diplomatic equation. If the Philippines were returned to Spain, wrote Henry Cabot Lodge, "the Democrats will unite in attacking us for doing so as false to freedom & humanity & we shall have no answer."[41]

Before he called the cabinet together, on the day when he heard from Spain, McKinley jotted down, for his own use, a draft of the American position: "As a condition to entering upon negotiations looking to peace, Spain must withdraw from Cuba and Porto Rico and such adjacent islands as are under her dominion. This requirement will admit of no negotiations." On the Philippine question the president employed open-ended language: "As to the Philippines, I am of the opinion, that with propriety and advantage they can be the subject of negotiation and whenever the Spanish gov't deems it, I will appoint Commissioners to this end." Significantly, he did not return to his mid-July remarks about an insurgent government under American protection with only a United States base at Manila. In the days of discussion that followed, McKinley steered the deliberations toward a result that he had already framed. He understood the political and diplomatic virtues of a governmental consensus on the Philippines, but he determined the precise shape that the cabinet's agreement would take.[42]

That body agreed with the president that Spain must relinquish Cuba and Puerto Rico. The Philippine question revealed that there were differences of opinion. Secretaries Bliss, Griggs, and Wilson favored taking all of the islands. Day, Gage, and Long would have settled for a naval base at Manila, or "a hitching post," as McKinley called it. Alger and Postmaster General Smith took little part in the talks. In the midst of one of the long parleys about the Philippines, the navy received a telegram from Dewey, reporting that the insurgents had become "aggressive and even threatening toward the Army." Under McKinley's guidance the cabinet voted narrowly in favor of leaving the ultimate status of the islands to the peace commission. Shortly thereafter, on August 1, 1898, General Merritt reported from Hong Kong: "It may be important [to] have my whole force before attacking if necessary to hold insurgents while we fight Spanish." The cabinet, said Secretary Wilson, read between the lines that the general might need a good many more soldiers. To ensure that the peace commission would do full justice to the insurgents and that it would take "abundant care of the spread of American powers," the administration decided that "no man will be put on that commission who is hostile to the acquisition of outside territory." McKinley was continuing the process, which he had begun in May, that led to annexation of the Philippines by the United States.[43]

Through the hours of meetings, McKinley made sure that the outcome would follow his scenario. He did not put Secretary Day's idea of a naval base at Manila to a vote, because as he said jokingly to his old friend, "I was afraid it would be carried!" When the laborious process of drafting and revision was over, Cortelyou wrote that the president's "guiding hand will be seen at every point in the negotiations." Cortelyou learned firsthand about McKinley's working methods on July 31. Closer to the center of power than ever before in his White House career, the young assistant secretary said to the president that the process of drafting a reply to Spain "was a good example of the development of a public paper under discussion—that there had been material changes by himself and the Cabinet since the first draft was made." After McKinley had shown him the July 26 memorandum, Cortelyou wrote in his diary: "These terms as thus stated by the President were exactly those which were finally transmitted to the Spanish Minister for Foreign Affairs, through the Ambassador of France."[44]

The final cabinet meeting took place on Saturday morning, July 30. As a draft of the American peace terms was being prepared, McKinley summoned Ambassador Cambon to the White House. When Cambon arrived at two o'clock, the president handed him the document, which asked Spain to relinquish all claims of sovereignty over Cuba and to cede Puerto Rico, other islands in the West Indies, and one of the Ladrone Islands in the Pacific. Finally, the paper stated that "the United States is entitled to occupy and will hold the city, bay, and harbor of Manila pending the conclusion of a treaty of peace, which shall determine the control, disposition, and government of the Philippines." Cambon attempted to explore the first two topics, but McKinley informed him: "My demands set forth in the first two articles do not admit of discussion." Only the Philippine question would be the subject of peace talks. The ambassador called them very hard terms, and he was able to achieve nothing more than a minor textual change in the article on the Philippines. McKinley remarked that Spain could have obtained easier terms in May, after the battle of Manila. If Madrid hesitated now, however, "Spain would necessarily be exposed to greater sacrifices." When Spain accepted the American offer, fighting would stop. Cambon departed at 5:30 P.M., and McKinley listened to the Marine Band that evening.[45]

Spain sent its answer to Cambon on August 1. It wondered whether other territorial indemnification might be substituted for Puerto Rico, and it said that the Philippine article was imprecise. Spain continued to assert claims to its permanent sovereignty in the islands. When Cambon returned to McKinley with this response, the president was inflexible on Puerto Rico. As to the Philippines, he said: "There is nothing determined *a priori* in my mind against Spain; likewise, I consider there is nothing decided against the United States." McKinley did agree to hold the peace conference in Paris, rather than Washington, which was his first choice. Cambon believed that he had obtained all that he could from the president and the secretary of state. "All vacillation will further aggravate the severity of the conditions," he warned Madrid.[46]

McKinley's diplomatic posture was steadfast despite revelations of the weakened condition of the army in Cuba, which undercut the American side of the negotiations in early August. During the two weeks after the surrender at Santiago the problem of the health of the troops, which was such a significant element in the parleys over the surrender, attracted less concern from the press and the War Department. Then the president was given alarming reports about conditions on two ships, the *Seneca* and the *Concho*, which were bringing troops to New York. An immediate investigation was ordered, and the War Department instructed Shafter to begin the partial evacuation of his troops. The next day, the general wired Washington that "at any time an epidemic of yellow fever is liable to occur" and advised "that the troops be moved as rapidly as possible whilst the sickness is of a mild type." The surgeon general of the army recommended that the troops move to higher ground, "where yellow fever is impossible." As Alger noted, "It is going to be a long job at best to get so many troops away." What the administration did not yet know was that sickness, malaria, and yellow fever had devastated Shafter's force.[47]

Faced with an order that he considered impossible to carry out, Shafter summoned his officers together. After opinion had been canvassed, the general told Corbin: "There is but one course to take, and that is to immediately transport the Fifth Corps and the detached regiments that came with it to the United States. If it is not done, I believe the death rate will be appalling." All he had left was an army of convalescents. With this description, Shafter sent statements from his medical officers and troop commanders which supported his decision. They did not reach Washington, but his comments were enough to impel the administration to "hurry other ships forward as rapidly as possible." Alger assured Shafter: "We are doing everything possible to relieve your gallant command."[48]

Since negotiations were in the balance, the White House hoped to sit on the news from Cuba until the evacuation of the soldiers could be begun. The press obtained a copy of the round robin from Shafter's officers, including General Joseph Wheeler, General

Leonard Wood, and Colonel Theodore Roosevelt. It stated: "The army is disabled by malarial fever to such an extent that its efficiency is destroyed and it is in a condition to be practically entirely destroyed by the epidemic of yellow fever sure to come in the near future." A separate letter from Roosevelt, written with his customary enthusiasm, said that the army was "ripe for dying like rotten sheep." On August 4 newspapers across the country carried the story in banner headlines.[49]

McKinley was furious. On August 5 he drafted a letter to Shafter that called the round robin "most unfortunate from every point of view" and said: "The publication of the letter makes the situation one of great difficulty. No soldier reading that report if ordered to Santiago but will feel that he is marching to certain death." Shafter's answer to the communications from Washington sought to smooth over the sensation that had been caused. The president was now aware that the management of the War Department had been maladroit. "Unless drastic measures are resorted to," wrote Cortelyou before the full weight of the round robin had been felt, "the Administration of that great branch of the federal service will be one of the few blots on the brilliant record made in the conduct of the war." Just how great a liability Alger had become, the president had yet to learn.[50]

That problem had to wait until the war had ended. Cambon brought the Spanish reply to McKinley's terms. Madrid could only accept the articles on Cuba and Puerto Rico. Hoping to salvage something in the Phillipines, Spain's Foreign Ministry argued that the government would have to secure the assent of the Cortes for any evacuation of Spanish territory before the treaty of peace had been concluded. This ploy irritated the president, who said: "I demanded of Spain the cession and consequently the immediate evacuation of the islands of Cuba and Porto Rico. Instead of a categorical acceptance, as was expected, the Spanish Government addresses me a note in which it invokes the necessity of obtaining the approbation of the Cortes. I can not lend myself to entering into these considerations of domestic government." With the talks in jeopardy, McKinley suggested that a protocol be drafted, setting out the American terms and specifiying when peace negotiations would start in Paris and when evacuation would commence in Cuba and Puerto Rico. At such time as Spain accepted, and if no approval of the Cortes or the Senate would be needed, the fighting would cease. Cambon warned Madrid again that McKinley would not alter these terms and that in the event of rejection, "Spain will

Ambassador Jules Cambon watching as Secretary William R. Day signs the Peace Protocol. Standing, left to right: Benjamin F. Montgomery, Eugene Thiébaut, Henry C. Corbin, John Bassett Moore, Alvey Adee, President McKinley, George B. Cortelyou, O. L. Pruden, Thomas Cridler, and Carl Loeffler. From the collections of the Library of Congress. This photograph was taken a few days after the actual signing.

have nothing more to expect from a conqueror resolved to procure all the profit possible from the advantages it has obtained." Spain had no option but to agree, and the government instructed Cambon to sign the protocol.[51]

The protocol was signed on Friday, August 12, on a rainy gloomy afternoon. News that the war had ended did not reach the Philippines until August 16. Three days earlier, after secret negotiations had been carried out with the Spanish commander in Manila, the American forces launched a combined land and naval assault on the city. The scenario that had been arranged between the defenders and the attackers was carried out, and after making a token resistance, Manila surrendered. Almost before it had commenced, the war with Spain was over, and the United States had prevailed on all fronts.

McKinley met the end of the war with a palpable sense of personal relief. "The days merge into each other," he remarked on July 30, and he told visitors that "the mental and physical strain of the last few months had been severe upon him." If his popularity had suffered with the coming of hostilities, the ensuing military events had restored it to the levels of 1897 or even higher. It was hardly surprising that Republican editors praised him; the remarks of foreign newspapers conveyed a judgment of greater respect. The president, said the *Spectator*, "is now by far the most influential personage in the United States."[52]

In conducting the Spanish-American War, McKinley had expanded the powers and authority of his office. Some months later, signing an order to shift American installations that lay outside the United States, he observed: "It seems odd to be directing the transfer of navy yards, naval stations &c in Cuba." He was able to accomplish these unprecedented activities because he was commander in chief, and the war power was the primary resource on which he relied in 1898. With the war behind him, McKinley approached the problems of peace with a confidence and assertiveness that would grow over the remaining years of his presidency. In bearing and manner, in action and policy, he would become something of an imperial tutor to the American people. "The true measure of duty is not what we like but what we ought to like," he wrote in August 1898. The political struggle over the Philippines during the rest of the year would reveal how much McKinley intended to shape and direct the way in which the United States would define its duty and would carry it out on the world stage.[53]

4

"DUTY DETERMINES DESTINY"

The most pressing political problem facing President McKinley at the close of the war was the growing clamor against Secretary Alger and the performance of the War Department. "There is a pretty general criticism here of the condition of the War Dept. in its Commissary and Medical branches," Secretary of the Navy Long was told, with the potential for "a very serious revulsion of public opinion against the administration's handling of the troops in Cuba." The partisan implications of the problem were obvious, and the Democrats intended to run in the fall on "the woeful failure of the Administration to provide proper food, sanitary conditions, clothing and hospital service from the beginning to the end of the war." From early August through the appointment of and the giving of instructions to the Commission to Investigate the Conduct of the War Department in September, the president moved to rectify the substantive difficulties within the government and simultaneously to contain the political danger.[1]

Criticism of Alger had appeared in mid May and had steadily mounted thereafter. As the revelations grew, even McKinley came under fire. "Alger is responsible for Algerism," said the *New York Evening Post*, "but McKinley is responsible for Alger." In two particular areas—the condition of the troops in Cuba and the management of the volunteer camps around the nation—the War Department and the secretary were found wanting.[2]

The army selected a site near Montauk Point, on Long Island, as the place for members of the Cuban expedition to recuperate after they returned home. When the "round robin" controversy broke, the camp was not yet ready to receive soldiers. Nonetheless, Shafter's men were ordered to be relieved as rapidly as possible and sent north. Between August 7 and August 25 the entire contingent that had fought at Santiago left Cuba. Work went forward at the rest camp, which was named Camp Wikoff after an officer killed at Santiago, but there were mix-ups and delays. The first troops, who arrived on August 14, found few tents, short rations, and inadequate hospitals. Newspapermen from New York City laid before a shocked country lurid and sometimes exaggerated accounts of suffering and neglect.

Conditions at Wikoff improved during the rest of August. The camp's commander—Joseph Wheeler—and Alger himself cut through red tape to obtain supplies and clothing. Their efforts, the hard work of the surgeon general, and an outpouring of private charity turned the installation into a more pleasant resting place for the men from Cuba. McKinley toured the camp on September 3 and told the press: "What I saw of the care of the sick in the hospitals by those in charge and by those noble women who are engaged in that work was especially gratifying to me."[3] Despite the administration's labors and the real achievements at Camp Wikoff, after its faltering start, the process of bringing the men back from Cuba was a public-relations disaster. Citizens saw soldiers on their way home, collapsing because of illness, or they read about visitors who could not find loved ones amid the confusion in the camp. Returning soldiers recounted vivid tales of the canned beef that formed part of their ration in Cuba. Never appetizing, the meat spoiled and sometimes contained foreign objects that disgusted those who ate it.

Equally damaging to Alger was the situation in the volunteer camps. Four primary bases—Chickamauga, Camp Alger near Washington, Jacksonville, and Tampa—served about 165,000 of the 200,000 men who had enlisted in the spring. Supply problems kept many of the soldiers from receiving clothing and equipment until the war was almost over. Because of poor locations, several of the camps became prime incubators of disease. Discipline broke down over the use of latrines at Chickamauga and Camp Alger. Conditions at the other camps were less onerous. With the approach of peace, however, the volunteers wanted to go home, and camp morale suffered. Simultaneously, cases of typhoid appeared, and the disease soon reached epidemic levels. Sick men crowded the hospitals, and then other cases had to be treated in the camps themselves. By the middle of August the army confronted a medical crisis.

The War Department's response to these difficulties was prompt. Hospital facilities expanded, and the quality of care rose. Troops were moved from the old camps to more healthful positions in higher places that were cooler and well watered. Better camp discipline replaced earlier laxness. These measures did not contribute directly to the abatement of the typhoid epidemic. After some weeks the disease ran its course among men who were susceptible to it. Some 2,500 officers and men died from typhoid, as compared with battle deaths of 281 officers and men. Better foresight and administration by the surgeon general, George H. Sternberg, could have reduced this grim total, as would have more careful supervision of their men by army officers. In large measure, however, typhoid fever and other diseases were inevitable, given the state of medical knowledge. In the minds of the American people, these considerations neither justified nor excused Secretary Alger's performance in office.

That Alger responded poorly to the criticism that surged around him is not surprising. His public chastisement of Roosevelt over the "round robin" only strengthened the conviction that the hero of the Rough Riders had been right. The secretary's official statements seemed to be belabored attempts to escape deserved blame. Since he had done nothing wrong, he would not step down, and he attributed the army's difficulties to circumstance rather than to errors in the conduct of the war. McKinley knew that there was a good deal of truth in Alger's defense. He told Cortelyou on August 23, after reading a letter that was critical of the secretary, that Alger "could not be responsible for many of the conditions at Santiago and other places; that if the food, medicines, etc., were not landed from the transports at Santiago it was the fault of the regular army officers who had charge of them and that Secy Alger could not know at the time what was going on." The president also realized, as did Alger, that the latter had taken the brunt of a public assault that might otherwise have struck the White House.[4]

If Alger could feel some resentment at how McKinley had treated him, the president also had grounds for a lessening of faith in his subordinate. Cortelyou did not overlook how Alger, in announcing administration decisions to newsmen, left the impression that he had originated the changes in official policy. Nor did Alger's caustic remarks about the president escape McKinley's attention. To limit the effect of Alger's troubles on the administration, then, he combined a public silence about the secretary with highly visible gestures to alleviate the army's problems. His trip to Camp Wikoff was one such act; another was the sending of a personal agent, a dietitian named Louise Hogan, to the camps in order to improve the quality of the food. When a New York newspaper editor wrote to the president in mid September about alleged starvation among American troops in Cuba, McKinley ordered an immediate probe, which revealed that there was no foundation for the charge. The most effective response, however, was the creation of a presidential commission to investigate the performance of Alger and his department.

The public outcry over the plight of the soldiers led inevitably to calls for a congressional inquiry. Such an investigation would have had a partisan dimension in an election year, and the president had little desire for an uncontrolled scrutiny of the war. Provocative statements from General Nelson A. Miles added to the inflammatory elements as McKinley vacationed during the first week of September. With characteristic adroitness, McKinley had begun to arrange for a process that he could supervise. He sent Secretary of Agriculture James Wilson to Alger to persuade Alger to ask the president "to appoint commission to report to you regarding the army and complaints concerning it." Wilson told Alger that internal reports by army officers would not satisfy the public, that the commission must have "men not in army life" who could fix "responsibility where it properly belongs." Alger agreed to Wilson's entreaties, and on September 8 he sent a letter to McKinley, asking that a board of five to seven "of the most distinguished soldiers and civilians" be named "to investigate thoroughly every bureau of the War Department." McKinley agreed to do this, and the Republican press applauded the decision to make a searching investigation.[5]

McKinley appointed his commission over the next several weeks. Some of the more prominent men whom he approached declined, but he pulled together a panel of two civilians and six soldiers who not only possessed expertise but would be fair. The chairman was General Grenville M. Dodge of Iowa, builder of the Union Pacific Railroad, who was a Civil War veteran and a Republican stalwart. The commission assembled in McKinley's office on September 26, 1898, to hear the president's instructions. "There has been in many quarters severe criticism of the conduct of the war with Spain," he told them; and he ordered a full investigation to establish "the truth or falsity of these accusations."[6] A few days later the Dodge Commission began its work. The hearings would later produce charges of scandal, in addition to a public controversy with General Miles. From its findings also came information that spurred reforms in the army. For the president, in the autumn of 1898, it deflected a formal congressional probe, and the Spanish-American War thus escaped that form of legislative scrutiny. By making the executive branch a kind of grand-jury prosecutor instead of a target, the commission extricated McKinley from a tight political corner; and this enabled him to deal with the elections and peace negotiations.

The prospects for the Republicans in the congressional elections seemed to have improved greatly since the worried predictions in early 1898. The war naturally evoked a nationalistic spirit, and as one midwesterner said in late April, "As a rule whatever arouses patriotism is good for us." Elections in Oregon in mid June appeared to signal a Republican resurgence on the Pacific Coast. At the end of the summer the organizers of the party's congressional campaign detected in the West and Midwest "a sentiment of general satisfaction" with the outcome of the war.[7]

Aware that the party in power ordinarily lost seats in an off year, Republicans looked to offset the Democratic attack on "Algerism" and the overconfidence in their own ranks. In New York, where scandals imperiled the GOP's dominance, the party machine of Senator Thomas C. Platt ran Theodore Roosevelt to supply a heroic candidate in place of the incumbent governor. The Republicans made an expansionist policy one of the keynotes of their national appeal.

McKinley took a close interest in the Republican effort. Assigning Postmaster General Charles Emory Smith to compile the campaign textbook, McKinley told him that he was "especially desirous" that the document reveal "the war situation as it existed." McKinley instinctively wanted the president to function as a party leader as well as a chief executive. Invitations also came in for the president to travel during the elections to Grand Army of the Republic meetings or to the various peace celebrations in the Midwest. To several of these inquiries, McKinley had his secretary send refusals because of the press of his duties. In late August, however, he decided to attend a peace jubilee in Omaha in October. Republicans immediately asked him to appear in closely contested districts in Iowa and other states along the route. The president said that "he would be entirely willing to do this not making political speeches, but discussing current events connected with the administration." Here was a significant departure from accepted political practice that became a precedent for the traveling White House of twentieth-century campaigns. Previously, most presidents had not campaigned for party candidates, even by implication; and the result for one who had, Andrew Johnson in 1866, was not encouraging. McKinley had been confined to Washington for a year, and he wished to renew his contacts with the public. If precedents were stretched on behalf of Republican victory, so much the better. He would also have an opportunity to mold public thinking on foreign policy. Secretary Cortelyou set in motion the arrangements for a presidential excursion.[8]

After his New Jersey vacation during the first week of September, McKinley faced a concentrated schedule of issues. In addition to the Alger controversy and the fall elections, the president had to supervise the military governments in Cuba and Puerto Rico. In the case of Puerto Rico the Spanish had departed on October 18, 1898, at which time the military occupation had commenced. The state of affairs in Cuba posed more delicate and perplexing questions.

The Cuban rebels contributed substantially to the defeat of the Spanish forces by doing reconnaisance work, by constructing trenches and supplying American troops, and, most important, by tying down large numbers of enemy reinforcements. Nonetheless, relations between the American and Cuban militaries worsened, and popular attitudes toward the erstwhile allies of the United States cooled to a near hostility. The Americans believed that the Cubans could not be trusted in combat or as co-workers. To men in Shafter's army they were a band of ill-equipped, undependable, larcenous fighters whose large contingent of black soldiers evoked the prevailing biases of North Americans. Public opinion in the United States largely agreed that McKinley had been right in not recognizing a Cuban republic.

While it readily accepted the aid that the Cuban forces provided, the administration did not accord the rebels any formal existence. They were not given an official role in the negotiations leading up to or in the surrender of Santiago de Cuba itself. In the process of notifying the Cuban junta about the adoption of the protocol with Spain, McKinley sought to make it merely a personal action. The Cubans extracted a concession that the message be transmitted to the president of their republic. At the same time, General Henry W. Lawton, who had replaced Shafter as the American military commander on the island, sought "definite instructions as to policy to be observed toward the Cuban army." The Cubans "still maintain their organization, are scattered through the country in vicinity of city, are threatening in their attitude, and keep the inhabitants stirred up and panicky by threats and acts of violence."

McKinley responded that "interference from any quarter" with the occupation by the United States would "not be permitted. The Cuban insurgents should be treated justly and liberally, but they, with all others, must recognize the military occupation and authority of the United States and the cessation of hostilities proclaimed by this Government."[9]

After the fighting had ended, Cuba was a devastated island. During the autumn of 1898 its inhabitants, with assistance from American relief agencies such as the Red Cross and the United States Army, brought some order out of the chaos and ruin that had accompanied rebellion and war. While the precise status of Cuba remained a topic for the peace talks, McKinley sent an agent to the island to gather information. Robert P. Porter, who had compiled a campaign biography of the Republican candidate in 1896, was a long-time publicist and government official with expertise in tariff matters. Named as a special commissioner to Puerto Rico and Cuba, Porter conducted hearings and interviewed residents. The recommendations that he made about trade relations between Cuba and the United States sought to raise a revenue for the islands without discriminating in favor of the occupying power. The precise form of government for the island, however, remained undecided. In November a Cuban delegation came to Washington to seek money to pay the insurgent army and other debts incurred during the rebellion. Negotiations ended inconclusively in mid December, and the emissaries reported that they had secured, at most, vague manifestations about the future policy of the United States. As McKinley said in his annual message, "Until there is complete tranquillity in the island and a stable government inaugurated military government will continue."[10]

The Philippines retained the president's primary attention in the autumn of 1898. New responsibilities overseas, in addition to the host of international issues that the war had left behind, convinced McKinley that he needed a secretary of state who had a background in diplomacy and a substantial reputation in world affairs. His old friend Judge Day, who was glad to serve on the peace commission, was equally ready to relinquish the duties at the State Department. To replace him, McKinley selected John Hay in August. After some initial hesitation because of his health, Hay accepted the diplomatic portfolio and took up his work on October 1.

John Milton Hay was sixty years old when he became secretary of state. A graduate of Brown University, he had been Abraham Lincoln's secretary and later had coauthored a multivolume biography of that president. Hay had been a diplomat, a journalist, and a successful man of letters. Financially secure, he was a reliable Republican contributor and early had supported McKinley. The new president sent him to London as ambassador, where Hay made a brilliant impression on his hosts as a promoter of Anglo-American friendship. McKinley found Hay's letters and dispatches both informative and shrewd. The ambassador's discreet flattery did not displease the president either. For McKinley's purposes, Hay was an ideal choice. The two men saw the world alike, and Hay would be an excellent instrument for the execution of McKinley's policies. The president told him at their first meeting that "he would not worry any more about the State Department." As usual, McKinley supervised and controlled the overall outlines of what Hay did.[11]

One of the most entertaining and interesting letter writers who ever ran the State Department, the witty, dapper, and bearded Hay left behind an abundance of documentary evidence on his public career. His name is indelibly linked with that verity of the nation's Asian policy, the Open Door, and he contributed much to the resolution of the longstanding problems with the British. Patient, discreet, and judicious, Hay deserves to stand in the front rank of secretaries of state. Sometimes, however, his tenure is examined as if McKinley were no more than a presidential appendix, present but superfluous, to the creative diplomat. Hay never made that error. He knew where the power resided and where the initiatives originated. Hay needed McKinley's firmness. Brilliant in statecraft, he possessed a disdain for patronage and a pathological distaste for the Senate in its constitutional role of advising and consenting to treaties. Left to himself, he would have had Congress in revolt. With McKinley to temper his failings and release his talents, Hay became the leading figure of the cabinet.

To accompany Judge Day to Paris, McKinley assembled a peace commission that symbolized his readiness to bend constitutional precedents. Whitelaw Reid received a place on it, not the ambassadorship to Great Britain that he coveted but an honor that was enough to placate him. The president also looked to the Supreme Court, but to his disappointment, Chief Justice Melville W. Fuller and Justice Edward D. White, both Democrats, declined. Ostensibly an independent branch of the government, the Supreme Court offered to McKinley the proper blend of judicial experience and political legitimacy that he sought in members of the peace commission.

Since senators would have to vote on the treaty that the commission negotiated, McKinley wanted to have several lawmakers among the peacemakers. He approached William Boyd Allison without success, and then persuaded Cushman K. Davis of Minnesota, an expansionist; William P. Frye of Maine, who shared Davis's opinions; and George Gray of Delaware, who disapproved of imperialism. Frye did not want to go, "but the President insisted that I should give a good excuse." The senator's desire "to fish and hunt" in the fall did not satisfy McKinley. As the commission's secretary, John Bassett Moore added a knowledge of international law and a firm grounding in McKinley's diplomatic objectives.[12]

McKinley was very sensitive to the role of the Senate in his plans for peace. He tried to induce George Frisbie Hoar to succeed Hay in London. Hoar's aversion for acquiring the Philippines was already public knowledge, and the appointment would have reduced the antiexpansionist bloc in the upper house. Hoar saw what the president's goal was, so he refused. Joseph Hodges Choate, a New York lawyer, filled the position. Senator William E. Chandler told McKinley that the president could not constitutionally name senators to a commission, upon whose product they would later vote. The president did not answer Chandler's protest, because he wanted the Senate to endorse what the negotiators achieved. More attuned to these legislative nuances than Woodrow Wilson two decades later, he was building a coalition in the Senate even before the peace treaty had been written.[13]

As the peace commissioners embarked for Paris, they required the president to instruct them about his intentions toward the Philippines. Since the signing of the protocol, McKinley had continued his policy of public indecision about the future of the islands while simultaneously shaping events aimed at full American control after the peace treaty was signed. His attitude emerged most clearly in relations with the Filipino insurgents.

After the assault on Manila, Aguinaldo told the American commanders that he wished to participate in the occupation of the city. General Merritt and Admiral Dewey asked Washington, "Is Government willing to use all means to make the natives submit to the authority of the United States?" Their message arrived on August 17, and the presidential response was firm: "The President directs that there must be no joint occupation with the insurgents." Since the United States was in the possession of Manila and its harbor, it had to preserve the peace and protect property in the archipelago. Therefore, McKinley ordered: "The insurgents and all others must recognize the military occupation and authority of the

United States and the cessation of hostilities proclaimed by the President. Use whatever means in your judgment are necessary to this end."[14]

With negotiations in Paris about to commence, the administration hoped to avoid a clash with the insurgents while at the same time withholding any formal recognition. The rebels themselves were divided about whether to ask for an American protectorate over an independent Philippines or to seek foreign recognition of Aguinaldo's government. Both potential adversaries wished, for the moment at least, to avoid a confrontation. The information that reached President McKinley indicated that, on the American side, the goal of establishing the army's authority in the Philippines was succeeding. Conveying information at the time that he was discussing Aguinaldo's hopes for a joint occupation of Manila, Merritt said: "Filipinos and their chief anxious to be friendly. Little confidence is to be placed in their professions. They are superior as a people than is generally represented; their leaders are mostly men of education and ability." This was the general's last policy statement. McKinley ordered him to Paris to confer with the peace commission. General Elwell S. Otis succeeded him on August 30, 1898. At the suggestion of John Bassett Moore, Otis was instructed on September 7 "to exert your influence during the suspension of hostilities between the United States and Spain to restrain insurgent hostilities against Spaniards, and, while maintaining a position of rightful supremacy as to the insurgents, to pursue, as far as possible, a conciliatory course toward all."[15]

General Otis's actions in early September seemed to comply with this presidential directive. In fact, his talks with Aguinaldo increased the tensions between the Americans and the Filipinos. He sent a formal response to the proposals that the insurgent leader made to Merritt in mid August. Should Aguinaldo not withdraw his troops from Manila by September 15, Otis warned, "I shall be obliged to resort to forcible action, and . . . my Government will hold you responsible for any unfortunate consequences that may ensue." Because of the negotiations with Aguinaldo, Otis's letter was kept private in Manila, and the withdrawal of the insurgent force was accomplished. The general could tell Corbin on September 16 that "based upon present indications," no additional American troops would be needed. The insurgent leaders were "in politics and army in excitable frame of mind, but better portion [are] amenable to reason, and desire to make approved reputation before civilized world." Otis's wire arrived in Washington on September 16, the day that McKinley met with the peace commission. He had reason to assume that his policy in the Philippines was not a source of so much intensifying friction with the insurgents that it might lead to open fighting.[16]

As he deliberated on the Philippines, the president received additional information to support his conviction that Spanish rule in the islands could not be successfully restored. The Japanese government, which conveyed this verdict, was equally cool to "a purely native Government, independent of external guarantees and guidance." Japan preferred that the United States take over the Philippines, but would, should Washington decline to accept sovereignty, help to set up "a suitable government for the territory," either by itself or with other powers. If the United States withdrew from the picture, a Philippine republic would confront, at the very least, serious threats to its existence from Japan and Germany.[17]

An American protectorate over the Philippines was an alternative possibility that McKinley weighed and then rejected. If the native government that appeared were only a façade for direct American supervision, it would be an awkward international entity. It it proved to be truly independent in its foreign policy, such a regime could easily involve the United States in commitments that the nation would not want to assume. A protectorate also involved a more complex and ambiguous obligation than did simple possession. For a president concerned about popular attitudes toward expansion and the country's willingness to support a colonial policy indefinitely, as McKinley was in September 1898, the equivocal nature of a protectorate type of obligation contributed to his dislike for the concept.

In semipublic appearances and in statements to visitors, McKinley maintained his noncommittal posture on the fate of the Philippines. To a visitor who was close to the German-American community, George Holls, he said in early September that "his mind was as yet a blank, so far as a decision upon the point of keeping or giving them back, was concerned." The president seemed to be impressed with the problem of sustaining "an army of occupation in a hot and unhealthy climate"; he talked of allowing Germany to have one of the islands or a part of the Ladrones; and he worried about whether public opinion would endorse holding the archipelago. A week later he asked a caller "whether it would not be just as well to keep only one Island in the Philippines, provided trade with the other Islands remained free and unrestricted, as for the United States to take all the Islands." As the peace commissioners prepared to meet with McKinley, the *New York Tribune* noted that the administration had not "gone beyond the determination to retain the whole of the island of Luzon." The president had decided "to establish at the outset" of the negotiations with Spain "the right of this Government to determine the fate of the islands and to make the conditions under which government shall be established there."[18]

McKinley, thus, instructed Day and his colleagues on September 16 that in the peace treaty the United States could not accept less than the island of Luzon as well as full commercial privileges in the trade of those parts of the islands that might remain with Spain. General Merritt was on his way to Paris to brief them about his own opinions and those of Admiral Dewey. The commissioners were warned that there was a need for promptness so that the Senate could consider the treaty before the Fifty-fifth Congress adjourned in March 1899.[19]

Most of the work in the White House on September 16 was devoted to conferences and ceremonies relating to the commission. Between meetings, however, another group of Americans came to see McKinley. At Saratoga, New York, on August 19 the National Civic Federation had held a conference on the direction that American foreign policy should be taking. When it met, opposition to expansionism had already emerged in Boston, where, on June 15, speakers such as Gamaliel Bradford and Moorfield Storey had criticized the prospect of an empire in Asia. Storey, Bradford, and Carl Schurz spoke at Saratoga against the acquisition of overseas possessions. The meeting adopted resolutions that were mildly critical of the administration, and it sent a delegation to see McKinley. Welcoming them in his graceful way, he expressed the hope that they had "come prepared to tell him just how much of the conquered territory should be retained, and just how much should be left within the control of Spain." The president's statement deflected the discussion into specific questions of policy such as "the expansion of our trade in the Orient" and away from a moral appraisal of imperialism. As McKinley's purposes became clearer, the opposition of Schurz and others would build.[20]

"The Peace Commission is now gone and that subject is off my mind," McKinley wrote on September 19. The Philippines did not step out of the public spotlight or leave the president's private deliberations while the peace negotiators went to Paris. At the end of the month, McKinley talked with, and received a lengthy memorandum from, Major General Francis V. Greene, who had been in the islands. Greene called Aguinaldo's form of government "a dictatorship of the familiar South American type," and he saw no reason to believe that it had any elements of stability. The insurgents did not have the hearty support of the Filipino people, whose ideal was "a Philippine republic under American protection, such as they have heard is to be granted to Cuba." The general concluded that, except for Aguinaldo, there was a consensus that "no native government can maintain itself without the active support and protection of a strong foreign government. This being admitted, it is difficult to see how any foreign government can give this protection without taking such an active part in the management of affairs as is practically equivalent to governing in its own name and for its own account."[21]

The day after Greene's memorandum had been submitted, representatives from Aguinaldo came to the White House. Felipe Agoncillo and Sixto Lopez gave the president a statement describing political conditions in their homeland. McKinley welcomed the two men "as citizens of the Philippine Islands" but specified that they had no political status. Agoncillo recounted what the Filipinos had endured from Spain, and he asserted that "they could never under any circumstances be content to be again placed in any manner or in any degree under the rule of Spain." He was going to Paris to address the peace commission, and the president invited him to present a memorandum of what he intended to say. On October 4 the document came in. It asked that the United States recognize Philippine independence and support principles of justice and human rights "in favor of the new nation which is rising logically in that part of the world in response to their well conceived and humanitarian action." The Aguinaldo regime sought to obtain the rights of a belligerent power and a part in the peace conference. The president and Assistant Secretary Adee offered no substantive comments on these claims. They not only reiterated instead that they did not recognize Lopez and Agoncillo "as agents of any governmental organization" but also denied the Filipinos' statements that Admiral Dewey, United States army officers, and diplomatic agents had engaged in de facto recognition of Aguinaldo in the campaign against Spain.[22]

Ten days later the president opened a western tour that took him through six states. During the two weeks of the trip he made fifty-seven public appearances, which included making major addresses at Omaha, St. Louis, and Chicago. The pressures of the Cuban crisis, the prosecution of the war, and the complexity of making peace had tied McKinley to the White House. It was good to be out among the people again. The mechanics of presidential tours were now more efficient as well, with Secretary Cortelyou in charge. From Cortelyou the reporters on the presidential train received advance copies of McKinley's formal addresses and stenographic reports of the numerous informal speeches that he made. A steady supply of bulletins went out to the wire services as the president crossed the nation's midsection. The crowds were large and enthusiastic. McKinley's popularity had swelled after the war, and he now reaped the ample applause that accompanies a successful war leader.

In the context of his Philippine policy, this speaking tour is usually depicted as the time when a pliable chief executive heard the voice of the people on the subject of expansion and returned to Washington with his doubts removed and his commitment to the acquisition of the Asian islands crystallized. The opposite was true. "He led public sentiment quite as much as public sentiment led him," Charles Emory Smith wrote later, "and the popular manifestations on that journey were in response to the keynotes he struck." The keynotes began early. At Cedar Rapids, Iowa, on October 11, he said, to great applause: "We can accept no terms of peace which shall not be in the interest of humanity." Later that day, at Secretary Wilson's home, Tama, he added: "We do not want to shirk a single responsibility that has been put upon us by the results of the war." What could that mean but the Philippines? At the Trans-Mississippi Exposition on October 12, he drove the point home with even greater force: "Shall we deny to ourselves what the rest of the world so freely and so justly accords to us?" The audience emitted a "general cry of 'no!'" He capped off his campaign at Chariton, Iowa, on his way east, the next day. "Territory sometimes comes to us when we go to war in a holy cause, and whenever it does the banner of liberty will float over it and bring, I trust, blessings and benefits to all the people."[23]

While on his junket, McKinley also advanced themes that could assist the Republicans in the fall campaign: "Business looks hopeful and assuring everywhere, and our credit balances show the progress which the country is making." Constantly he emphasized that the war had brought the North and the South into closer union: "Never was a people so united in purpose, in heart, in sympathy, and in love as the American people to-day." But throughout he returned to the cadences of foreign policy. At the Auditorium in Chicago, he proclaimed on October 18: "My countrymen, the currents of destiny flow through the hearts of the people. Who will check them? Who will divert them? Who will stop them? And the movements of men, planned and designed by the Master of men, will never be interrupted by the American people." In his native Ohio, in Columbus, where he had been governor, he remarked: "We know what our country is now in its territory, but we do not know what it may be in the near future."[24]

McKinley's use of what Theodore Roosevelt called the bully pulpit is still one of his least recognized contributions to the emergence of the modern presidency. Outside the precise political context of October 1898, the speeches seem stuffed with generalities. When read in tandem with the epochal events of that critical year, they become masterful examples of how an adroit leader can set the terms of a public discussion in his own favor. McKinley had for the moment wrapped the Philippine decision in the folds of prosperity, patriotism, and the national interest. "Duty determines destiny," the president had said; but it was he who prescribed the nature of that duty.[25]

The trip immediately made a favorable impact upon Republican fortunes in the campaign. "We have not as yet been able to satisfy ourselves what will be the result in the next House," concluded the chairman of the party's Congressional Committee on October 15. The committee had no money, and after the excitement of the 1896 race, apathy seemed to be the most dangerous obstacle to the GOP's chances. Then McKinley went west. On his return, said one paper, he received a "continuous ovation" as he passed through Indiana and Ohio. In late October, Republican spokesmen revised downward their predictions of potential party losses so as to minimize the effect of the off-year contest. Meanwhile, the Democrats lacked decisive issues. The opposition was still divided over silver, had no consensus on imperialism, and found that McKinley had deflated the "Algerism" outcry.[26]

On the day of the election the Democrats gained fifty seats in the House. Many of the defeated were Populist incumbents whose party had waned since 1896. Republican losses totaled nineteen, but the party retained a twenty-two-vote edge in the House. Roosevelt achieved a narrow victory in New York, and the GOP added six seats to its Senate count. Expecting the customary reversal, the Republicans experienced bearable setbacks. "You have pulled us through with your own strength," John Hay informed McKinley; "this makes the work for 1900 simple and easy." Most important, the administration could look forward to controlling both houses of Congress after March 1899.[27]

While the president's trip and the political campaign progressed, the peace commissioners opened their talks with their Spanish counterparts. At an early informal meeting, the president of the Spanish delegation said that he hoped the Americans would remember that "you are the victors, and we are the vanquished; that magnanimity becomes the conqueror," and that Spain therefore might "hope for liberal terms from the American Government." The Spanish knew that they had little chance of prevailing at the peace table. Once again, they hoped that prolonged discussions would show public opinion in Spain that Cuba and the Philippines had not been easily relinquished. In the interval, the elections might produce gains for the Democrats and presumably a softer American position. More time would also make it possible for the army to return from Cuba and for the troops to be discharged peacefully.[28]

The American commissioners differed only over the Philippines. On the other points at issue they adhered closely to the terms of the August protocol and to McKinley's instructions. By means of the telegraph wire the president guided the negotiations on the side of the United States, as daily reports in cipher kept him informed of shifts in the situation. The talks began on October 1. The Spanish attempted at the outset to restore the status quo in the Philippines as it had existed before the protocol was signed. The Americans refused to accept what would have been essentially a renunciation of their sovereignty in the islands. Proceedings then turned to the protocol. Spain proposed, at the meeting of October 7, 1898, that the United States accept sovereignty over Cuba and agree as well to assume responsibility for the debts that Spain had incurred.

Both the American representatives in Paris and William McKinley rejected the ideas regarding Cuban sovereignty and debt. "We must carry out the spirit and letter of the resolution of Congress," the president cabled on October 13. The commissioners believed that their adversaries were hoping for a breakdown in the talks that might justify making an appeal to the European powers to arbitrate the question. The issue of Cuban debt dominated the ensuing two weeks of meetings, private consultations, and sessions on American strategy. Then, on October 21, Spain rejected the argument of the United States. They again proposed that the Americans not only take sovereignty over Cuba but also assume the island's debts. Day and his colleagues agreed that "unless otherwise instructed we shall reject these articles and insist upon our articles in terms of protocol and press matters on these points to a conclusion." To this communication, McKinley replied that he fully approved of the stand of the commission.[29]

At the conference session on October 24 the Americans, through Day, said: "We cannot accept *anything* which attaches the sovereignty or the debt of Cuba to the United States." Later in the deliberations he inquired whether the Spanish "would not consent to any articles relating to Cuba and Puerto Rico which did not embody or carry with them in some form an assumption of the Cuban debt, either by the United States or by Cuba or by both." The Spanish replied that they wanted the Cuban debt "somewhere" in the ultimate document. Day then repeated his question about whether Spain would reject a treaty that omitted the debt, and the commissioners from Madrid sought time for a consultation. The Americans, wrote Reid in his diary, believed "that the Spaniards would yield."[30]

To push matters to that end, Reid hinted, in a private conversation with one of the Spaniards, that concessions on the Cuban issue might stimulate American financial generosity with regard to the Philippine problem. Spain could "find something either in territory or debt which might seem to their people at home like a concession." Whether Reid's overture was decisive is unclear. It certainly impelled Spain in a direction that it would have taken in any case. On October 26 Spain agreed to the American articles, reflecting the "exact language of the protocol," that dealt with Cuba, Puerto Rico, and Guam. Only the Philippines now stood in the way of the treaty.[31]

When they were not occupied with formal meetings with the Spanish or in the inescapable round of ceremonial entertainments, the commissioners received information about, and debated the ultimate disposition of, the Philippines. They heard from John Foreman, who had written on the islands and their history; from Commander R. B. Bradford, their naval attaché, who had just visited the islands; and from General Merritt. The president also sent the Greene memorandum and a report on the talks with Agoncillo. When a message came from Admiral Dewey in mid October, that too went on to Paris. "The natives appear unable to govern," he said, and he underlined the importance of deciding what to do with the archipelago as soon as possible, so that a strong government could be established. The commissioners did not allow Agoncillo to appear before them to present the insurgents' case.[32]

After weighing the evidence and discussing the issue among themselves, the commissioners were still divided. Senator Gray wanted as little of the islands as was feasible; there was "no place for colonial administration or government of subject people in [the] American system." Day believed that the national commitment should be kept within bounds, and he recommended the taking of Luzon and other islands that would safeguard American naval interests. Davis, Frye, and Reid generally favored taking all the Philippines, because there was "no natural place for dividing" them. On October 25 the commission, as a body, asked McKinley for "early consideration and explicit instructions" about what they should now ask of Spain.[33]

The formal record of McKinley's response is now well established. In an instruction that the president drafted personally, Secretary Hay wired on October 28 that "grave as are the responsibilities and unforeseen as are the difficulties which are before us, the President can see but one plain path of duty—the acceptance of the archipelago." American public opinion agreed that "the people of the Philippines, whatever else is done, must be liberated from Spanish domination." The Spanish could not give the islands to another power, and the exercise of joint sovereignty by the United States and a third power was ruled out. "We must either hold them or turn them back to Spain." Moved "by the single consideration of duty and humanity," McKinley ordered the commissioners to demand all the Philippines from the Spanish.[34]

McKinley's instructions of October 28 were the logical culmination, indeed the inevitable result, of the policy that he had pursued since the tentative news of Dewey's victory had been learned on May 2. A subsequent presidential statement, allegedly made thirteen months afterward, in November 1899, introduced a religious element into his decision-making on the Philippines. This has provided critics of his action with powerful reasons to depict him as either a hypocrite or a bemused instrument of the Almighty. A delegation from the Methodist Episcopal Church visited the White House on November 21, 1899. As they began to leave, so one of them recalled, McKinley asked them to wait and then said "just a word about the Philippine business."

Recapitulating his predicament over what to do about these unexpected spoils of war, he confessed "I did not know what to do with them." He asked for "counsel from all sides" but obtained "little help." Then he turned to religion. "I walked the floor of the White House night after night until midnight; and I am not ashamed to tell you, gentlemen, that I went down on my knees and prayed Almighty God for light and guidance more than one night. And one night late it came to me this way—I don't know how it was, but it came." Giving the islands back to Spain "would be cowardly and dishonorable." To transfer them to France or Germany "would be bad business and discreditable." The Filipinos were "unfit for self-government—and they would soon have anarchy and misrule over there worse than Spain's was." The president concluded "that there was nothing left for us to do but to take them all, and to educate the Filipinos, and uplift and civilize and Christianize them, and by God's grace do the very best we could by them, as our fellow-men for whom Christ also died." Sleep came to McKinley, and the next day he gave instructions that the Philippines be put on his office map of the United States, "and there they will stay while I am president."[35]

McKinley's biographers have accepted the accuracy of this remarkable revelation without making much of an effort to verify its authenticity. The reporter of the interview, James F. Rusling, published it in January 1903, more than three years after the Methodists had gone to the White House. Beyond Rusling's good memory of his visit and the president's exact words, there is the coincidence in Rusling's memoir of the Civil War, published in 1899, where Abraham Lincoln said to him in 1863 after the battle of Gettysburg: "I went to my room one day and got down on my knees and prayed Almighty God for victory at Gettysburg." For Lincoln too, "after thus wrestling with the Almighty in prayer, I don't know how it was, and it is not for me to explain but, somehow or other, a sweet comfort crept into my soul" that the Union would win at Gettysburg. Rusling was very fortunate in being able to bring out the theological side of two presidents, but, in the face of two such similar accounts, there is the possibility that Rusling improved on McKinley's words with a device that had served him once before.[36]

If the religious references are left out, the rest of McKinley's remarks become a lucid outline of the considerations that confronted the president in the autumn of 1898. He was making just such outlines to other visitors in November 1899. To the editor of a German-American newspaper, McKinley read from his October 28, 1898, dispatch, and then said: "You see thus I have been carried further and further by the events." He added that "Providence had made us guardians of the group of islands." Faced with mounting criticism from anti-imperialists in the autumn of 1899, McKinley was leaking information to friends and critics in order to offset attacks on his Philippine policy. His comments to the Methodists have at best a modest value as a description of his thoughts a year before they were made; their famed religious context is very questionable. Without that rhetorical excess, his statements become only part of a presidential counterattack, directed at the impending campaign year of 1900, rather than a revealing or essential clue to McKinley's internal thought process during the Philippine crisis.[37]

McKinley's message to Paris rested the American claim to the Philippines on the right of conquest. The commissioners believed that Spain could make a strong argument on this point, since Manila was not taken until after the protocol was signed. Some concessions to the Spanish would be prudent so that they could satisfy their domestic opponents with tangible evidence of their courage. In the process, a resumption of the fighting would be avoided. Senator Frye suggested to the president on October 30 that a payment of from ten to twenty million dollars might help secure a treaty for the United States. Hay reported McKinley's reply that if the commissioners thought that the United States should pay "a reasonable sum of money to cover peace improvements which are fairly chargeable to us under established precedents, he will give cheerful concurrence." At the meeting with the Spanish on October 31 the United States demand for all the Philippines was made.[38]

The Spanish held out for several weeks, hoping still that the congressional elections, friendly powers in Europe, or some happy incident might avert their humiliation. In mid November, McKinley repeated his insistence on taking all the islands, and the American negotiators echoed his firmness. They said, on November 21, that the islands must be ceded and that a payment of $20 million would be made. Spain and her diplomats sought a way out of their predicament, but they found none. On November 28 they agreed to the American terms. There were still many details to be discussed in the remaining two weeks of negotiations. The disposition of Spanish islands in the Pacific brought the Germans into the picture briefly. In the end the treaty that was signed on December 10, 1898, largely corresponded to the terms of the protocol and to McKinley's October instructions. The United States acquired the Philippines, Puerto Rico, and the island of Guam; Spain gave up Cuba, but not its debt, and received the $20 million payment.

The signing of the Peace of Paris concluded one significant phase of McKinley's Philippine strategy. He now had to steer the document through the Senate in the lame-duck session that concluded on March 4, 1899. The Republicans would be in firmer control of the upper house when the new Congress convened in December 1899, and the president could have called a special session in early March with strong assurances that the treaty would be approved. McKinley did not want to have the lawmakers in session to confront the colonial issue. Though the fight in the short session would be a tough one, McKinley desired prompt action on the treaty, and he shaped his course in December 1898 in expectation of the battle ahead.

Celebrations to mark the end of the war drew McKinley southward in the middle of the month. Ostensibly nonpolitical, the week-long trip to Georgia, Alabama, and South Carolina enabled him to promote, among the constituents of Democratic senators, sentiment in favor of expansionism. A series of eleven speeches also allowed McKinley to arouse patriotic feelings through references to how the war had eased animosities between the North and the South. "Sectional feeling no longer holds back the love we bear each other," he told the Georgia Legislature on December 14. The president stood when "Dixie" was played, and he wore a badge of gray. To these marks of sectional accord, the southern audiences responded with enthusiastic applause.

Before a crowd at the Auditorium in Atlanta on December 15, McKinley reported that the flag had been "planted in two hemispheres, and there it remains the symbol of liberty and law, of peace and progress. Who will withdraw from the people over whom it floats its protecting folds? Who will haul it down?" Two days later, at Savannah, he returned to that theme: "If, following the clear precepts of duty, territory falls to us, and the welfare of an alien people requires our guidance and protection, who will shrink from the responsibility, grave though it may be?" Toward the end of the junket, at Augusta on December 19, he summed up his message: "There are no divisions now. We stood united before a foreign foe. We will stand united until every triumph of that war has been made permanent. [Applause]." Disgruntled critics said that the "popular clamor" was "entirely sweeping him off his feet as it has many other men." The acclaim was not swaying the president; he was evoking the applause with the same dexterity that had moved the Midwest in October.[39]

Insulated from immediate popular pressure because of the six-year terms of its members, the Senate received the treaty in early January. If all ninety senators were present, the treaty would require sixty votes for approval. There were fifty Republicans, of all persuasions, including western silver men; thirty-five Democrats; and five Populists or Independents. Complicating McKinley's task were the probable defections of Senator George Frisbie Hoar of Massachusetts and Eugene Hale of Maine. To win the treaty fight, the administration had not only to hold the rest of the Republican ranks firm but also to gain some votes from the Democrats and Populists. The president took personal charge of the protreaty drive in December and January. In the Senate the nominal leader of the ratification effort, Senator Davis, played a smaller part than did Senators Nelson Aldrich, Stephen B. Elkins, and Henry Cabot Lodge.

The McKinley administration also possessed the political initiative in this legislative battle, and it pressed this advantage. The new Congress would be more strongly Republican; therefore, delaying until after March 4, while it would be awkward for the president, would also do little for the opposition. Above all, the forces favoring the treaty argued that the peace settlement was a fact. Rejection of the document would only embarrass the chief executive and the United States abroad. Henry Cabot Lodge said to his fellow senators on January 24, 1899: "The President can not be sent back across the Atlantic in the person of his commissioners, hat in hand, to say to Spain with bated breath, 'I am here in obedience to the mandate of a minority of one-third of the Senate to tell you that we have been too victorious, and that you have yielded us too much, and that I am very sorry that I took the Philippines from you.' "[40]

The White House deployed other weapons in the contest over the treaty. It encouraged state legislatures to pass resolutions endorsing the pact. Such pressure from constituents helped to move California's senator, George C. Perkins, out of the doubtful column and into the protreaty side. Two southerners who voted as the administration desired, John L. McLaurin of South Carolina and Samuel D. McEnery of Louisiana, obtained a large voice in the allocation of patronage in their states; but Senator George Gray's federal judgeship, to which the president named him in 1899, was less a reward for his vote in the Senate than for his service in Paris. In the case of Senator Richard Kenney of Delaware, however, there were intimations that relief from his legal problems in his home state was linked with his support for the treaty.

Opponents of the treaty were less successful in pulling together the thirty-one senators that they needed in order to beat the administration. Divided counsels prevented the emergence of a clear, well-focused antitreaty strategy. William Jennings Bryan, who had just resigned from the army commission that he had held during the war, said to reporters on December 13, 1898: "It will be easier, I think, to end the war at once by ratifying the treaty, and then deal with the subject in our own way." Bryan was reluctant to turn the diplomatic task back over to McKinley; he thought that the Democrats would suffer if the treaty were not ratified and if violence were to occur in the Philippines; and he knew that sentiment for the pact was strong among western silver Democrats. His support for the treaty did not furnish the votes to approve it, but his position underlined and increased the disunity among the partisan enemies of the administration.[41]

The alternatives that the antitreaty senators presented against McKinley's clear goal of approving the peace with Spain further revealed the lack of cohesion in the opposition camp. One bloc of senators wanted to make changes in the language of the document on the Philippines by renegotiating the entire treaty. The champion of this point of view was Arthur P. Gorman of Maryland, who became the leader of the antitreaty forces in the Senate. Gorman thought that consistency on the issue of imperialism demanded that the Democrats oppose the treaty as it had come from Paris. Another group, with Augustus O. Bacon of Georgia as their spokesman, hoped to obtain a congressional resolution that would promise future independence to the Philippines.

Despite the inherent advantages that the administration possessed, the battle over the treaty in January 1899 was tense and close. Debate, which began in executive session on January 4, went on throughout the month. The Republicans asserted publicly that they had the votes for ratification and were ready to ballot at any time. In private, one of them conceded that there was "no certainty of our getting the necessary number of votes for the treaty on February 6th, although I hope that we shall do so." On January 25 the two sides agreed to take the vote on February 6. "The administration," said Senator Hoar, "is moving Heaven and earth, to say nothing of some other places, to detach individual Senators from the opposition, and we shall be very anxious until the thing is settled." As January ended, administration senators wavered over the prospects for the treaty. "Day before yesterday," wrote Senator Charles W. Fairbanks of Indiana, "it seemed there would be no doubt of ratification, but yesterday the tide seemed to be against us."[42]

Only a few days before the voting was to take place, the uncertainty continued. White House forces believed that they were within two votes of the sixty they required. They hoped to find the necessary votes among the four undecided senators. February 6 fell on a Monday, and on Saturday evening, February 4, cables came to the president reporting that fighting between American soldiers and Filipinos had begun. In his diary, Cortelyou wrote that McKinley sat well back in his chair and finally said: "It is always the unexpected that happens, at least in my case. How foolish these people are. This means the ratification of the treaty; the people will understand now, the people will insist upon its ratification."[43]

The administration knew that the military situation in the Philippines was deteriorating in early 1899. McKinley had hoped to obtain approval of the peace treaty and thereby to convince the Filipinos that American sovereignty could not be successfully resisted. Able first to control events in Paris and then in Washington from October 1898 through February 1899, the president found that developments in the Philippines were less amenable to his management during this period. Information came to him slowly and sketchily, and the reports that he gathered about relations between the Americans and the natives of the islands often conveyed an erroneous optimism. Still, the basic problem that divided the two sides was not susceptible to negotiation. McKinley intended to establish America's dominance in the Philippines; Aguinaldo and his forces wanted to limit and restrain the influence of the United States in order to preserve as much independence as they could.

The uneasy accommodation between the Filipino soldiers and their American rivals showed increasing strain during the autumn of 1898. In mid October, General Otis insisted on further withdrawals of Aguinaldo's men from positions near Manila. The insurgents complied after making some protests, and the general told Washington: "Our relations now [are] apparently friendly." That judgment was in error. Aguinaldo was consolidating the control that his men exercised in the islands; he was approaching foreign governments, especially Japan, about diplomatic recognition; and he was capitalizing on resentment against the Americans to win popular support for the revolution. The propensity of the United States soldiers for labeling Filipinos as "niggers" and for bullying their way through the towns made the insurgents' case against the invaders very plausible. By November 13 Otis recognized that his predicament was worsening. "Prudence dictates that all troops here and soon to arrive be retained," he told Washington; "Aguinaldo ambitious, acting with unscrupulous members of cabinet and advisers, cries independence, secretly assert Americans must be driven out." The general concluded: "Many important problems constantly arising here but no serious difficulty anticipated. Necessary to maintain adequate force to meet possible emergencies."[44]

As the negotiations in Paris approached an end, the administration explored the requirements for maintaining American power in the Philippines. Otis estimated that, in the event of Filipino resistance, he would need twenty-five thousand men. A week later the president asked Dewey and Otis for advice about what force and equipment would be necessary in the Philippine Islands. McKinley asserted that the government of the islands would, of necessity, "be by the Army and the Navy for some time to come," and he wanted "as kind and beneficent a government as possible given to the people." Otis responded on December 8 that the Americans should occupy the port of Iloilo, which was still under Spanish control, and he further recommended that judicial and governmental machinery be established quickly, with Filipinos in key positions. On December 14 he requested orders to seize Iloilo.[45]

McKinley's absence in the South caused his answer to be delayed until December 21: "The President directs that you send necessary troops to Iloilo to preserve the peace and protect life and property. It is most important that there should be no conflict with the insurgents. Be conciliatory but firm." Otis received this message on December 23, and troops left three days later. By the time they arrived, the Filipinos had control of the port; and as 1898 ended, the insurgents had a visible presence in extensive portions of the archipelago outside of Manila.[46]

While the military position of the United States worsened, McKinley pushed his political program to establish American ascendancy. On December 27 he sent instructions to Otis that he had prepared six days earlier. The president claimed that Dewey's victory and the surrender of Manila had "practically effected the conquest of the Philippine Islands and the suspension of Spanish sovereignty therein." The peace treaty, though it had not yet been ratified, ceded to the United States "the future control, disposition, and government of the Philippine Islands." Accordingly, McKinley maintained that "the actual occupation and administration of the entire group of the Philippine Islands becomes immediately necessary," and he wanted military government "extended with all possible dispatch to the whole of the ceded territory." If, a few weeks earlier, McKinley had felt "strange" about exercising presidential authority outside the United States, his letter to Otis seems to indicate that he had overcome such qualms.

The substance of McKinley's instructions underscored the need "to announce and proclaim in the most public manner that we come, not as invaders or conquerors, but as friends, to protect the natives in their homes, in their employments, and in their personal and religious rights." American rule would be established "with firmness if need be, but without severity so far as may be possible." The municipal laws of the Philippines would be continued, insofar as military government would allow; private property should be respected; and foreign trade would be resumed. Above all, Otis was told, the military should strive to show the Filipinos that "the mission of the United States is one of benevolent assimilation, substituting the mild sway of justice and right for arbitrary rule."[47]

Events in the Philippines now outpaced McKinley's directives. The War Department ordered Otis on December 29 "to occupy all strategic points in the island possible before the insurgents get possession of them." Otis, who replied that the Filipinos occupied most of the military posts outside Luzon, concluded: "Situation requires delicate manipulation, and our troops here can not be widely scattered at present." Washington answered that Otis should not "prosecute the occupation too rapidly, but proceed with great prudence, avoiding conflict if possible, and only resort to force as the last extremity." To avoid arousing suspicions among the inhabitants of the islands, Otis released a digest of McKinley's instructions that played down the president's claims to sovereignty and stressed the benevolent purposes of the United States. This maneuver failed when the American commander at Iloilo released the complete text of the president's letter. Aguinaldo angrily threatened to begin fighting if the Americans extended their control over the Philippines.[48]

When, on January 8, Otis reported the reaction to McKinley's orders and also the uneasy conditions between Filipinos and United States soldiers, McKinley sent him another elaboration of the administration's attitude: "Am most desirous that conflict be avoided. . . . Time given the insurgents can not hurt us and must weaken and discourage them. They will come to see our benevolent purpose and recognize that before we can give their people good government our sovereignty must be complete and unquestioned." Otis should continue the talks that he was having with Filipino leaders, and the president offered to aid in these negotiations and in the establishment of a workable civil-military government.[49]

At the end of McKinley's second year in the White House the commission device had become one of the characteristic features of his presidency. He had used commissioners on the bimetallic initiative; he had formed the Joint High Commission to negotiate with the British; and he had enlisted lawmakers to survey the political and economic needs of newly annexed Hawaii. Now he turned again to the same idea for the Philippines. On the commission that he selected on January 19, 1899, were Charles Denby, a Democrat and one-time minister to China; Dean C. Worcester, a zoologist from the University of Michigan; and Jacob Gould Schurman, president of Cornell University.

Worcester had called on the president in order to share with him the experiences gained from research trips in the Philippines. Worcester's ideas about the islands were influencing McKinley's policy by late December 1898. Schurman told the president, who asked him to head the commission, that he did not favor taking the Philippines. "Oh, . . . that need not trouble you," McKinley declared; "I didn't want the Philippine Islands, either; and in the protocol to the treaty I left myself free not to take them, but—in the end there was no alternative." Schurman acceded to the president's request, and the civilian commissioners left the United States on January 31, 1899.[50]

The commissioners could not have any immediate effect on the tense situation in the Philippines. Both sides sought to settle their differences in conference for two weeks after McKinley's message of January 8. Six meetings occurred, in which it became obvious that the Americans would insist on a recognition of United States sovereignty, while the Filipinos, at least those who represented Aguinaldo, wanted the independence of the islands to be accepted before his government would discuss the precise form of an American protectorate. Negotiations broke off on January 29, 1899. Where American and Filipino forces confronted each other, the atmosphere grew sharp and inflammable. Hostilities began on February 4, when Americans and Filipinos fired on each other. "Insurgents have inaugurated general engagement yesterday night which is continued to-day," was the form in which McKinley first received the news.[51]

The Senate voted on the treaty in midafternoon on February 6, 1899. Contrary to McKinley's forecast, news of the fighting at Manila did not make the task of the administration forces any easier. With three hours to go, the treaty was still two votes short of the necessary two-thirds. Senator McLaurin of South Carolina, induced in part by promises of patronage, then moved into the affirmative column. Senator McEnery of Louisiana followed when the Republican leadership agreed to endorse his resolution that the United States had no intention of annexing the Philippines as part of the United States. Senator John P. Jones of Nevada added an aye vote after the initial roll call. The final vote was 57 to 27, one more vote than was needed for ratification.

The effects of the battle echoed for several days. The Senate passed the McEnery resolution by four votes, but it was defeated in the House. Opponents of the treaty pushed a resolution of Senator Bacon's which promised Philippine independence. Because some administration senators were absent, there was a tie vote of 29 to 29 on the resolution. Vice-President Hobart cast the deciding vote against the proposal. The vote on this resolution provides a misleading picture of the administration's legislative strength during the winter of 1899. Had the full Senate been present, Bacon's idea would have been overwhelmingly beaten.

The greatest victory in the fight over the treaty was McKinley's. Other causes helped the treaty. Bryan's stance divided the opposition; if he had enthusiastically opposed the treaty, it would probably have been beaten. The anti-imperialist coalition in the Senate was a fragile and fractious one, and it did not offer any attractive alternative to what the administration proposed. The president made the difference. From Dewey's victory onward, he guided events so that American acquisition of the Philippines became logical and, to politicians and the people, inevitable.

Once the fighting had ended, while there was still a United States presence in the Philippines, McKinley constantly kept in mind, as he conducted affairs, that there would eventually be a Senate battle over the peace treaty. His idea of selecting senators to serve on the peace commission was an innovation that involved a merging of the legislative and executive branches for the president's own ends. Modern communications enabled McKinley, as they had in his fighting of the war, to participate directly in the peace-making process in Paris. Simultaneously, in October he exploited the publicity weapons of a strong executive during his midwestern tour to shape public opinion. He performed with equal skill in his December swing through the South. In the treaty fight itself, he returned to the techniques of close management and personal participation that he had shown in handling the Cuban and Hawaiian issues. There are few better examples, before the time of Franklin D. Roosevelt, of the exercise of presidential power in foreign affairs than McKinley's successful effort to obtain Senate approval for the Peace of Paris.

The war in the Philippines was the most unpleasant legacy of the dramatic occurrences of 1898. The future of the islands was the primary topic of McKinley's address to the Home Market Club in Boston on February 16. Almost six thousand guests and listeners heard the president deliver one of the most effective speeches of his life. Of the American commitment in the Philippines he said: "It is a trust we have not sought; it is a trust from which we will not flinch." He reviewed the options at the peace negotiations and decided that "there was but one alternative, and that was either Spain or the United States in the Philippines." As to the Filipinos, Americans had, as their sole purpose, to safeguard "the welfare and happiness and the rights of the inhabitants of the Philippine Islands." An expression of opinion from the inhabitants of the islands on the rule of the United States would, however, have to wait. "It is not a good time for the liberator to submit important questions concerning liberty and government to the liberated while they are engaged in shooting down their rescuers."

With the war behind them, McKinley went on, the American people now had the future of the Philippines before them. Until Congress acted with regard to the islands, the president would give "to the people thereof peace and order and beneficent government." McKinley underlined that "neither their aspirations nor ours can be realized until our authority is acknowledged and unquestioned." In the speech he made no specific promises about the Filipinos in the years ahead, but he sought to defuse anti-imperialist charges: "No imperial designs lurk in the American mind. They are alien to American sentiment, thought, and purpose. Our priceless principles undergo no change under a tropical sun. They go with the flag." In his peroration, McKinley invoked a picture that was not limited "by the blood-stained trenches around Manila—where every red drop, whether from the veins of an American soldier or a misguided Filipino, is anguish to my heart." He looked instead to "the broad range of future years," to the Philippines as "a land of plenty and increasing possibilities; a people redeemed from savage indolence and habits, devoted to the arts of peace, in touch with commerce and trade of all nations, enjoying the blessings of freedom, of civil and religious liberty, of education, and of homes, and whose children and children's children shall for ages hence bless the American republic because it emancipated and redeemed their fatherland, and set them in the pathway of the world's best civilization."[52]

Exactly one year before, McKinley had learned of the destruction of the *Maine*. In those twelve months the United States had struggled for peace, had won the war with Spain, and had gained an empire. At the center of the process that changed the nation's history was William McKinley. He transformed the presidential office from its late-nineteenth-century weakness into a recognizable prototype of its present-day form. The Home Market speech revealed what the developments of the Spanish-American War foreshadowed. From the seedbed of the House of Representatives, the governorship of Ohio, and the campaign of 1896 had appeared the first modern president. During his remaining years in the White House, McKinley would build upon and expand the legacy of power and authority that then passed to Theodore Roosevelt and Woodrow Wilson.

5

"THE PERIOD OF EXCLUSIVENESS IS PAST"

The issues that grew out of the Spanish-American War dominated the remaining years of McKinley's presidency. The controversy about the War Department ran on through the first half of 1899 even as the administration dealt with the insurrection in the Philippines and the transition from war to peace in Cuba. To attain the larger goal of American dominance in the Caribbean and North America, there were negotiations with Great Britain and Canada that had as their ultimate prize the building of a canal across Central America. In Asia the involvement with China deepened as the administration promulgated the Open Door policy and sent troops there in response to the Boxer Rebellion of 1900.

"You have got a great load in the management of the War Department," an old friend told McKinley in March 1899. That judgment was valid.[1] Between December 1898 and March 1899, the administration waged a difficult struggle in Congress to secure and sustain an expanded army after the war with Spain had ended. The final bill was a compromise. The army obtained a force of sixty-five thousand regulars and thirty-five thousand two-year recruits, and it achieved as well a real advance toward greater federal control of the armed services.

The administration also survived a controversy over the testimony of General Miles before the Dodge Commission, which had been established to investigate the conduct of the war. Initially the commission's work in October and November 1898 lessened the political damage. Its wide-ranging hearings did not produce sensational revelations. Then, on December 12, 1898, Miles told the panel and the press that he was looking into whether the army's beef had contained chemicals that caused it to spoil. The charge that the army had used "embalmed beef" became one of the most enduring historical memories of the war.

In fact, the reality was far less sensational. A product of the major meat-packing houses, the meat was, for the most part, an adequate ration when cooked. When eaten raw in the field, it had a bland, unappetizing flavor, and it spoiled quickly. Some of the cans contained foreign elements and dead insects; so the meat was highly unpopular with the soldiers. Unsuitable for the tropics, the canned roast beef was a mistake, but it was an error of judgment, not an example of corruption or conspiracy. Both the Dodge Commission and a court of inquiry found in 1899 that Miles, in his statements to the newspapers, had exaggerated about the quality of the meat given to the soldiers.

The full report of the Dodge Commission was critical of Secretary Alger's leadership. "The general administration of the War Department" lacked, it said, "that complete grasp of the situation which was essential to the highest efficiency and discipline of the army."[2] Nonetheless the secretary remained in office through the first half of 1899. The president wanted Alger to resign voluntarily. To fire him would be to admit tacitly that there was some substance to the charges against the War Department. Preferring, in personal relations, to use finesse rather than to confront, McKinley attempted to outwait his cabinet officer.

Alger's involvement in Michigan state politics in the summer of 1899 was the occasion for his ouster. His ambitions to fill a seat in the United States Senate became entangled with the antiadministration rhetoric of Governor Hazen Pingree, a bitter critic of McKinley's foreign policy. After Pingree made negative statements about the president's Philippine decisions, Alger had to go. Working through Vice-President Garret A. Hobart, McKinley obtained the secretary's resignation on July 19, 1899. From the beginning, Alger's membership in McKinley's cabinet had been a mistake. The secretary of war had done his best during the conflict, and many of his problems were not of his making or were beyond his control. But he stayed too long, once the war had ended, and the president moved too slowly in obtaining Alger's resignation.

To succeed Alger, McKinley wanted a man who could deal with the administrative and colonial side of the War Department's work in 1899. For the "good legal and governmental man" he needed, the president chose Elihu Root of New York, a corporation lawyer. In late July, Root received a call from an emissary of the White House: "The President directs me to say to you that he wishes you to take the position of Secretary of War." Root answered: "I know nothing about war, I know nothing about the army." The reply came back: "President McKinley directs me to say that he is not looking for any one who knows anything about war or for any one who knows anything about the army; he has got to have a lawyer to direct the government of these Spanish islands, and you are the lawyer he wants."[3] Root became one of McKinley's best appointees.

The conflict in the Philippines presented the most vexing problem for the administration once the war with Spain was officially over. During the early months of fighting, the army could only hold onto the position that it already had. As the size of the forces in the islands grew in 1899, the American situation improved. When the dry season began in mid October, the commander, General Elwell S. Otis, launched an offensive across Luzon. The Americans were able to destroy the Filipino army as an effective combat instrument for regular warfare. What McKinley did not know, and what General Otis failed to recognize, was that Emilio Aguinaldo and his advisors had decided to shift from conventional warfare to guerilla tactics.

While the military situation was developing in 1899, McKinley pursued the policy of "benevolent assimilation" he had proclaimed in late 1898. To convince the Filipinos of the good intentions of the Americans, the army sought to establish a fair judicial and legal system, to build sanitation projects, to open schools, and to set up municipal and local governments. Such tactics were not, sadly, always followed, and they did not—because of the nationalism, propaganda, and terrorism of the insurgents—prove effective in and of themselves.

Benevolence occurred within a framework of paternalism toward the Filipinos. Believing the reports of the army and his civilian commissioners, McKinley did not think that Aguinaldo's insurrection was a genuine manifestation of popular sentiment in the islands. This position perhaps underestimated the support that Aguinaldo, his government, and the independence movement enjoyed.

Through the Philippine Commission, with Jacob Gould Schurman as its president, the administration sought in 1899 to create a framework of government. Promising "an enlightened system," a proclamation of April 4, 1899, offered "the largest measure of home rule and the amplest liberty consonant" with American sovereignty. The declaration led to guarded talks with some insurgents, but McKinley, for legal and political reasons, would not yield on the maintenance of the supremacy of the United States. First the Filipinos must yield; then further conversations could proceed over the degree to which they might have "the largest measure of local self-government consistent with peace and good order."[4]

The commission reflected this position in its two reports of November 1899 and February 1900. "There is no course open to us now except the prosecution of the war until the insurgents are reduced to submission." McKinley, drawing upon the conclusions of Schurman and his colleagues, intended, as the insurrection appeared to wind down, to form a civil government for the Philippines. In January 1900 the president selected a second commission, with a federal judge, William Howard Taft, as its chairman, "to go there and establish civil government."[5] The commission would first set up municipal bodies; provisional governments would then follow. The commission was given broad legislative authority to tax and to create an educational system, a judiciary, and a civil service. It left for the Philippines on April 17, 1900.

While American rule in the islands solidified, opposition to imperialism continued at home. The main vehicle of protest was the Anti-Imperialist League, which claimed a national membership of thirty thousand. It included among its supporters such prominent figures as Carl Schurz, Moorfield Storey, and Edward Atkinson. The intemperate Atkinson sent antiwar literature to soldiers in the field, and protests were made when the army tried to interrupt the flow of pamphlets. Some newsmen on the battlefields claimed the army was also covering up bad news.

Critics focused on the retention of volunteer detachments to fight the war in Asia. It seemed likely that the state of mind of the volunteers would become a political issue in the off-year elections, which would provide hints about 1900. By the end of August 1899 the volunteer regiments were on their way home. While on vacation from the heat of Washington, McKinley attended receptions that were given for the returning volunteers. He said of those troops: "They did not stack arms. They did not run away. They were not serving the insurgents in the Philippines or their sympathizers at home." With American sovereignty under attack, there would "be no useless parley, no pause, until the insurrection is suppressed, and American authority acknowledged and established."[6] The president reiterated this theme on a tour of the Midwest in the fall of 1899 and again in the election year of 1900.

Throughout their protest campaign, the anti-imperialists argued that American military policy was cruel and barbarous. The question of atrocities being committed in the war aroused a large public controversy during the administrations of McKinley and Theodore Roosevelt; and the Vietnam War, seven decades later, revived the issues as participants in the quarrel over American actions in Southeast Asia looked back to the Philippines and accused the McKinley administration of having committed genocide on a scale unmatched until the Nazi horrors of the Second World War.

The charges that the United States had a conscious policy of killing Filipinos indiscriminantly between 1899 and 1902 and that it, in fact, slaughtered several million people are untrue.[7] The American presence did not produce—through combat, atrocities, or other causes—any disastrous effects on the Filipino population as a whole. But what of atrocities and war crimes? Such actions were never the stated policy of the United States government, nor were they ever officially condoned. The army court-martialed far more violators than it covered up. There was no killing of prisoners on an organized basis, nor were the wounded mistreated as a rule. In the day-to-day rigors of combat, however, American soldiers did commit acts that violated the rules of war and the regulations of their own army. The United States, which had condemned "Weylerism" in Cuba, found itself employing similar tactics in a colonial war of its own. The unhappy outcome of the Philippine imbroglio was a potent warning against engaging in similar ventures in the future.

In the presidential election of 1900, McKinley effectively countered the efforts of William Jennings Bryan, who was the Democratic candidate again, to make the Philippines the decisive issue. Bryan called for a stable government in the islands, with independence and an American protectorate to follow. In his letter accepting the Republican nomination, the president said that self-government would come "when they are ready for it and as rapidly as they are ready for it." The protectorate idea, he believed, would draw the nation "into their troubles without the power of preventing them." McKinley skillfully narrowed the policy differences with Bryan, while undermining the idea of a protectorate.[8]

After his reelection the president obtained from Congress in early March 1901 legislation that accorded to him, in explicit terms, the power to govern the Philippines after the insurrection had been suppressed. Meanwhile, the Taft Commission had exercised legislative power since September 1, 1900. For the majority of Filipinos who wanted peace under American sovereignty, Taft argued that there should be an effort made to train them in self-government, while real power should be kept in American hands. The commission promulgated laws for municipal government, for provincial government, and for the creation of a system of public schools. Taft also worked to overcome jurisdictional disputes with the American military commander, General Arthur MacArthur.

On the strictly military aspect of Philippine affairs, the insurgent strategy of guerilla resistance was in full operation throughout 1900. American promises of amnesty largely failed to sway the Filipinos. After the election, the army adopted harsher tactics, which were embodied in a declaration of martial law for what were called unpacified areas of the islands. Once Congress had confirmed his authority to move forward with civil government for the Philippines, McKinley directed that Taft assume full executive powers there. The explicit transfer of power from soldiers to civilians occurred on July 4, 1901. Meanwhile, the insurrection received a heavy setback when Aguinaldo was captured on March 23.

The insurgents fought on for another year before the United States declared that the archipelago had been pacified. Other resistance sputtered on for several years. By the time that McKinley died, in September 1901, American supremacy in the Philippines seemed to be an accomplished fact. What the president had achieved would not impress Americans in the twentieth century, sensitive as they had become to the postponement of Filipino independence. Misguided, by present-day standards, and certainly paternalistic, McKinley was, in his way, a sincere friend of the Philippines and, with foreign rule inevitable, the best external ruler the islands could have had after Spain departed.

The fighting in the Philippines gave the administration its greatest concern in 1899/1900, but the fate of Cuba aroused nearly as much worry. In shaping Cuban policy so as to avoid fighting between Americans and their former allies, McKinley had to reckon not only with the previous decisions of Congress about the island but also with the international situation and the state of American public opinion. Most important in this process was the Teller Amendment of April 1898, in which the United States had renounced any intention of retaining Cuba after the island had been pacified. Though the government found the amendment an irksome restraint on its freedom of action, McKinley made it clear that he would honor the congressional pledge.

At the same time, the president was anxious that Cuba not once again become a source of diplomatic difficulty. The government that emerged must be strong enough to maintain its existence while remaining friendly with and in the orbit of the United States. If the Cubans would not accept such a relationship, the United States would have to create political constraints on a newly independent island when the American army relinquished control.

The military government that began its work on January 1, 1899, had to be a success if the United States were to achieve its policy objectives. During the first seven months of the year, until Elihu Root became secretary of war, the army repaired the ravages of war but achieved less striking results with the political revival of the island. Cubans were fed, their medical needs were attended to, sanitation projects went forward, and a system of schools was created. In Havana, garbage collection, disease control, and food allocation proceeded at an accelerated pace. By the end of 1899, moreover, only about eleven thousand American soldiers remained in Cuba.

The administration avoided one potentially dangerous problem during these months. The Cuban army was dispersed, with its members receiving $75 each. On a less visible level, of course, the Cubans bridled at a regime that did not know their language, that labeled some of them as dagoes, and that imposed upon them laws to prohibit the ringing of church bells, gambling, or the opening of taverns on Sunday.

In Congress, too, McKinley encountered challenges to his authority in regard to Cuba. The Foraker Amendment of February 1899 to the army appropriations bill barred the granting of franchises or concessions to American entrepreneurs for the duration of the occupation. Like the Teller Amendment, the measure was a self-imposed restraint on American action. It reduced economic activity, which might have encouraged annexationist sentiment, but it also retarded projects that could have benefited the Cubans.

By mid 1899, confusion characterized the administration's policy with regard to Cuba. The military leadership had moved slowly to create the political institutions on the island, and McKinley had not made clear his middle position between annexation and complete independence. The selection of Elihu Root provided the president with the proper instrument for administering Cuba. Working together, they put General Leonard Wood in charge of the island in December 1899, and McKinley told Wood: "I want you to go down there to get the people ready for a republican form of government." At the same time, Root proclaimed that American control in Cuba would last only as long as necessary to create a government "which shall really represent the people of Cuba and be able to maintain order and discharge its international obligation." McKinley struck the same theme in his 1899 annual message: "The new Cuba yet to arise from the ashes of the past must needs be bound to us by ties of singular intimacy and strength if its enduring welfare is to be assured."[9]

Wood moved rapidly to implement McKinley's orders. "By the instructions of my government, we are marching toward independence," he told Cuban leaders.[10] After a census and municipal elections, the election of delegates for a constitutional convention was set for September 3, 1900. The nationalists on the island prevailed, controlling the largest bloc of votes at the convention, which began on November 5, 1900. The American government expected this body to recognize Washington's right to intervene in the new country's affairs in order to protect it from internal chaos or foreign domination. The administration also thought that the Cubans should grant naval stations to the United States. Worried about foreign influences in the Caribbean—especially a German presence—and dubious regarding the Cubans' ability to manage their own affairs, McKinley and his advisors believed that the United States had to possess the formal, recognized ability to prevent domestic disruption and outside intrusion.

Throughout December 1900 and into January 1901, the Cuban delegates were reluctant to do what the McKinley administration desired. They wanted a prompt end to the military government, and they expected tariff concessions from the United States. In response the White House and Congress began to formulate what was to become the Platt Amendment. Root asked Secretary Hay to consider whether the United States should compel Cuba to recognize that America had a right to intervene in order to preserve Cuba's independence and stability. Further, the administration might bar a Cuban government from concluding with a foreign power any treaty that might infringe the island's sovereignty; it might also insist that the United States had a right to have naval bases on Cuba. For a time the administration considered summoning a special session of Congress to deal with this issue.[11]

In late January, Congress began to move. Senator Orville H. Platt of Connecticut used Root's ideas in the Committee on Cuban

Relations to draft a memorandum that McKinley approved on February 8, 1901. "That is exactly what I want," said the president. Within three days the wording of the Platt Amendment to the army appropriation bill was set. Cuba could not impair its independence through a treaty with a foreign power; its government could not assume public debts beyond its capacity to repay; and the United States would be able to intervene "for the preservation of Cuban independence and the maintenance of a stable government." Congressional debate on the amendment occurred in late February and concluded with its passage by the House on March 1.[12] Legislative action in this way, under McKinley's guidance and with support from anti-imperialists, mirrored a general agreement in Washington that the Platt Amendment was an appropriate means of safeguarding the nation's stake in Cuba.

The Cubans reacted to the amendment with immediate unhappiness. As one of their leaders commented: "Should we concede this, there will be born a government resting upon a supposition of incapacity."[13] The people of the island demonstrated against the amendment, and petitions were circulated in opposition to it. McKinley and Root responded with private assurances that the United States did not intend constant "intermeddling or interference with the affairs of a Cuban Government."[14] They did insist, however, that the constitutional convention accept the Platt Amendment as it was written. Finally, the Cubans did so on June 12, 1901. In May 1902, after McKinley's death, Cuba became independent. If the Platt Amendment was relevant to the international situation between 1898 and 1902, during which time the fears of German intrusion were probably overdrawn, the amendment lost much of its rationale thereafter and became only a source of Cuban-American discord. The effort to free Cuba from Spanish rule had culminated in de facto American dominance by the time McKinley's presidency concluded.

Trade relations with the island of Puerto Rico also revealed the economic and constitutional problems that the war had brought. In September 1899 a hurricane killed nearly three thousand people and devastated the coffee crop that furnished the bulk of the revenues for the island. To alleviate the disaster, Secretary Root advocated, in his annual report, the complete removal of any tariff barriers between the United States and Puerto Rico. McKinley concurred in his annual message: "Our plain duty is to abolish all customs tariffs between the United States and Puerto Rico and give her products free access to our markets."[15]

McKinley and Root had blundered. Their stance on the Puerto Rico tariff had undercut the protective system of the Republicans and had called into question whether Congress had the authority to make rules for the new possessions. The president seemed to be adopting the position of the Democrats that the Philippines, Hawaii, and Puerto Rico had now been brought within the United States and that tariff regulations therefore did not apply to goods imported from them to the mainland. American beet-sugar growers, the sugar industry generally, and tobacco growers were not likely to be pleased.

As the constitutional and political implications emerged, McKinley's stance shifted. In late January 1900 he disclosed that he would agree "that a small or nominal rate of duty shall be imposed on imports from the island." The president regarded the constitutional question as "paramount—for upon the proposition that Congress had the right to govern the Islands by legislation with a 'free hand,' depends the success of our colonial policy—especially in the Philippines."[16]

McKinley's constitutional position was clear. His political prospects were less solid. Having come out for free trade originally, he was supporting by late February a compromise tariff that would place a 15 percent duty on Puerto Rican products for a two-year period and would use the revenues on the island itself. Some House Republicans still supported McKinley's original posture, and it took intense White House pressure to get the bill through that body on February 28.

Over the next month, the president negotiated with the Senate to achieve a satisfactory result there. By the last week in March, a further compromise emerged. The 15 percent duty remained, in general, and concessions were made to remove duties on food and other products in order to conciliate legislators who still backed free trade. The Senate acted favorably on April 4, and the House went along a week later. The issue of the Puerto Rican tariff aroused strong feelings in the spring of 1900 and revived talk of McKinley's indecisiveness. It had not been one of his best episodes, but his initial motives were right and the political damage was slight and temporary. A year later, in the Insular Cases, the Supreme Court resolved the issue of whether the Constitution covered the Philippines and Puerto Rico. The justices decided that the new possessions belonged to the United States and were therefore under the authority of Congress but that their inhabitants were not United

States citizens. The ruling upheld the position that the administration had taken regarding Puerto Rico in 1900.

Because of the ambition of the United States to confirm its ascendancy in the Caribbean, the need to clear the way for the building of an isthmian canal was one of the most significant consequences of the Spanish-American War. First the United States had to revise or dispense with the Clayton-Bulwer Treaty of 1850. That document denied to Great Britain and the United States exclusive power over a canal area and specified that a canal could not be fortified. The treaty also provided mutual guarantees of the neutrality of a canal. Unless the treaty were renegotiated, the United States could not construct an American canal. The British, and especially the Canadians, hoped that the desire for the canal might induce Washington to make concessions about other North American issues, especially the Alaska boundary.

Further complicating these matters were those who favored different routes across the Central American isthmus. The route across Nicaragua had the most proponents in the 1890s, but it faced competition from the advocates of a Panamanian canal. During the war the battleship *Oregon* had steamed ten thousand miles around Cape Horn from the Pacific to join the Atlantic Fleet. Arriving too late to join the major battle off Cuba, the *Oregon* had dramatized the need for a canal and for revision of the Clayton-Bulwer Treaty. In his annual message of 1898, McKinley urged Congress to act; and Secretary Hay began work on a draft treaty with the British ambassador, Sir Julian Pauncefote.

Events in Congress slowed negotiations with Britain and shifted the emphasis toward a route across Panama. In January 1899, lawmakers considered a bill to guarantee the financing of a canal in Nicaragua. The Senate approved it overwhelmingly, even though it called for a canal that the United States would construct and control and said nothing on the obvious conflict with the Clayton-Bulwer Treaty. Seeking American concessions and concerned about placating Canada, Britain elected not to go ahead with a draft treaty in the winter of 1899. Meanwhile, Congress decided not to adopt the Nicaraguan route, creating instead a commission to study all isthmian routes.

When Congress reconvened in December 1899, Great Britain was on the brink of the Boer War in South Africa. With the American legislators ready to move ahead unilaterally, the British were not in a position to alienate the United States. On February 5, 1900, the Hay-Pauncefote Treaty was signed. The British agreed that the United States could build its canal; the Americans pledged to keep the waterway open, even in wartime, to all nations, and not to fortify it. Hay expected quick ratification. Instead, senatorial opposition developed to the provisions of the treaty, and it became necessary to postpone a vote on the pact until after the presidential election. At the same time, the House and then a Senate committee approved a bill for an American canal in Nicaragua.

The Senate, when it took up the Hay-Pauncefote Treaty in December 1900, added an amendment that allowed the United States to fortify the canal for its own defense or to keep order, abrogated the Clayton-Bulwer Treaty, and dropped language that invited other powers to take part in the pact. Despite McKinley's reservations, the Senate ratified the treaty as amended on December 20, 1900. The British rejected the treaty in March 1901. Repressing his distaste for his senatorial opponents and borrowing some of McKinley's techniques, Hay now reshaped a new treaty. He consulted with leading senators and then tailored his work so as to secure a two-thirds majority. For the British he offered wording that formally abrogated the Clayton-Bulwer Treaty, applied the neutrality provisions only to the United States, and dropped the Senate amendment without limiting the right of the nation to defend the canal in wartime. On April 25, 1901, the new draft was sent to the British. Much negotiation lay ahead, but Hay had made possible the eventual signing and ratification of the second Hay-Pauncefote Treaty in November and December 1901. From then on, Theodore Roosevelt took over the process of obtaining the canal zone and building the Panama Canal for the United States.

The most enduring diplomatic initiative that the McKinley administration produced after the war was the Open Door policy, which was launched in September 1899. The acquisition of the Philippines and the expanded role of the United States in Asia intensified the existing concern, both in the government and in the private sector, about the fate of China in 1898. Addressing the peace commissioners on September 16, 1898, about the Philippines, McKinley also said: "Incidental to our tenure in the Philippines is the commercial opportunity to which American statesmanship can not be indifferent. It is just to use every legitimate means for the enlargement of American trade; but we seek no advantages in the Orient which are not common to all. Asking only the open door for ourselves, we are ready to accord the open door to others."[17]

Extensive public support existed for a more forceful policy in China. The problem lay in determining the best means to use in accomplishing the desired ends, and the administration spent the twelve months after September 1898 waiting for the right moment to shape a China policy. The options that were open were relatively limited. The Philippine insurrection tied down the available military resources that might have sustained direct American action in China, and the domestic controversy over imperialism, as well as the national tradition of noninvolvement in the affairs of other countries, made overt intervention in China politically questionable. The power with which the country might logically cooperate was Great Britain; but such an alliance, even if informal and tacit, also posed risks for the Republicans from Democratic critics of the president. In addition, London entered into an agreement with Russia in April 1899 that divided up railroad spheres in China, a decision indicating that Britain was committed to achieving areas of influence that would be comparable to those of its European rivals.

Events in midsummer 1899 persuaded the president and the secretary of state that the United States should set forth its own attitude toward the future of China, as the European powers continued to establish spheres of influence and leases on the mainland. On August 11, Czar Nicholas II issued a ukase declaring that the port of Talienwan in Manchurian territory, which was under Russian control, would be open to the merchant ships of all nations. The Russian action suggested that that nation and Great Britain would be receptive to an assertion of United States policy about the Open Door.

To prepare the case for the United States, Hay turned to an old friend and long-time student of Asian affairs, William W. Rockhill, who was the director of the Bureau of American Republics. That summer, Rockhill was corresponding with a British friend, Alfred Hippisley, about China's problems. Hippisley did not represent the views of the British government but was, rather, an official of the Chinese Maritime Customs Service who believed that the United States should preserve the Open Door in China.

Rockhill and Hippisley exchanged ideas and data throughout July and August, and they kept Hay informed of their thoughts. On August 24, Hay asked Rockhill to draft instructions to ambassadors in Great Britain, Germany, Russia, and France. Approved by McKinley on September 2, the Open Door notes went out to the American diplomats in the four major countries on September 6. The Open Door notes sought to have the powers that were involved, which also came to include Italy and Japan, accept three American assumptions. In China the nations that were already there would not interfere with each other's sphere of interest. Chinese tariff duties would apply within areas of foreign influence, and the Chinese would collect the customs duties. Finally, there would be no discriminatory harbor dues or railroad rates within the respective spheres of influence.

If these proposals were agreed to, the United States would retain many commercial advantages which might otherwise disappear under the economic system that the powers were imposing in China. The Open Door notes also attempted to preserve for the Chinese some part of their government's power and their nation's integrity. At the same time, the administration was responding to and restraining the imperialistic surge in China through an independent policy that cooperated with the British in substance, answered the felt needs of the business community, and yet circumvented any need for consultation with the Senate.

The powers reacted to the initiative in ways that fell far short of acceptance of the American position. Great Britain most nearly approached agreement with the proposal. The Russians were essentially negative, and the Germans, French, Italians, and Japanese said, as the British and Russians had, that they would agree only if all the other nations did. In March 1900 Hay proceeded to announce that the replies from the six nations satisfied him and the American government. The secretary had put the best possible face on the diplomatic situation, and his public posture enjoyed wide domestic support.

By the time the Open Door policy was announced, there were more ominous developments in China. At the root of the Boxer Rebellion lay antiforeign sentiments. The secret associations that called themselves Righteous and Harmonious Fists drew upon the support of farmers, who were confronted with drought, and upon the backing of some elements of the court of the Chinese empress. The rebels moved out from their base in North China to menace the foreigners in the legations at Peking in May 1900. In early June, several hundred foreign troops arrived in Peking, but a relief force of fifteen hundred was repulsed. By June 13 the Chinese capital was isolated as the Boxers cut the telegraph lines.

The administration's first responsibility was for the safety of the Americans under siege. Initially it tried to act independently of the other powers, but it eventually had to cooperate with the western nations. Despite the demands connected with subduing the Philippine insurrection, the army moved some twenty-five hundred men into the China Relief Expedition in June 1900. All this occurred without congressional action because the president believed that he had enough authority, under the war power, to dispatch troops to China. Introduction of American forces into a country with which the nation was not at war measured how far the Spanish-American conflict and its consequences had enhanced presidential power.

Events seemed to justify McKinley's decisions when the siege of Peking was lifted on August 14. The army and navy, in tandem with the other powers, had helped to liberate the foreigners in the capital. As the United States worked to accomplish the freeing of the western diplomats, the administration moved to prevent the crisis from ending in the breakup of China. On July 3 Hay sent the second Open Door note to American representatives in what was a significant elaboration of earlier policy on the subject. The purpose of the United States was to "preserve Chinese territorial and administrative entity, protect all rights guaranteed to friendly powers by treaty and international law, and safeguard for the world the principle of equal and impartial trade with all parts of the Chinese Empire."[18]

In the aftermath of the lifting of the Boxer siege and the enunciation of the expanded Open Door policy, the president had to contend with the consequences of the broadened American commitment in Asia. At some point, McKinley may have wanted, as he put it, a "slice" of China; but during the summer of 1900 he did not, in public, find much attraction in an American military presence of even a semipermanent kind. As he wrote to Hay on September 14: "I know of no way to get out but to come out."[19] By that month the number of American soldiers in China was decreasing, and the White House was pushing for a settlement that would recognize as much of Chinese authority and diplomatic influence as possible.

After the election of 1900 the United States explored in a preliminary way whether it might be possible for the navy to secure a base on the Chinese coast. The Japanese expressed their opposition, which closed out the matter for the time being. In shaping a final resolution to the aftermath of the Boxer crisis, the administration acted as a moderating influence. The terms that were given to China in late December 1900 included less stringent provisions than the other powers had envisioned. During the negotiations that followed, the United States reduced its military commitment in China, pressed for low payments from Peking as indemnities, and accepted its share of the financial settlement, with the understanding that eventually some of the money would go back to China. William Rockhill conducted the parleys, which resulted in a protocol signed on September 7, one day after McKinley was shot. The president died having established the principles of the Open Door and China's territorial integrity as two major precepts of the nation's foreign policy in Asia.

McKinley was assassinated while making a speaking trip to Buffalo, New York, in September 1901. He came to the Pan American Exposition to talk on trade relations and economic policy. In the course of his address on September 5, 1901, he observed that "the period of exclusiveness is past" and that "isolation is no longer possible or desirable." In addition to his primary emphasis on tariff reciprocity, he called for a larger merchant marine, completion of an isthmian canal, and telegraph cables to Hawaii and the Philippines. "Our interest is in concord, not conflict," the president concluded. "Our real eminence rests in the victories of peace, not those of war."[20] Nonetheless, McKinley's words revealed how widely the nation had adopted global interests in the wake of the Spanish-American War.

The next afternoon, while standing in a receiving line at the Temple of Music, McKinley was shot in the stomach. He died eight days later from gangrene and infection. McKinley, John Hay said in his eulogy in 1902, "showed in his life how a citizen should live, and in his last hour taught us how a gentleman could die."[21] Despite the warmth and love that McKinley evoked in the American people, their memory of him faded rapidly. By the time of World War I the picture of McKinley as president, which had been so vivid in 1901, had grown fuzzy and vague.

Historical scholarship after 1920 created the McKinley that textbooks and general accounts have made so familiar. His handling of the Cuban crisis came in for particular criticism, but his entire administration was dismissed as little more than a mediocre prelude to the energy and vigor of Theodore Roosevelt's eight years in office. It is now possible to correct these misconceptions.

The Spanish-American War was not the result of presidential weakness or cowardice in the face of public hysteria. McKinley sought to persuade Spain to relinquish Cuba peacefully and then turned to war when it became apparent that Madrid would never acquiesce. His diplomacy in 1897/98 was tenacious, coherent, and courageous. He took the nation into war with the presidential prerogatives in foreign affairs strong and undamaged.

During the war, McKinley directed the American military effort and the diplomacy that brought territorial acquisitions and peace. His guiding role as a war leader facilitated the accretion of power in the executive department and in the federal government generally. An unprepared nation did not perform with efficiency in every aspect, as the record of the War Department showed, but in the later stages of the fighting, the army functioned with greater success than is often realized. The navy's record throughout was "one of remarkable achievement."[22] The striking result of the brief conflict with Spain was how broadly and creatively McKinley used his power as commander in chief.

The process of making peace with Spain—involving, as it did, American annexation of the Philippines—and of securing ratification of the resulting treaty in the Senate underscored McKinley's expansive view of presidential power. From the sending of senators on the peace commission to the personal supervision of the terms of the negotiation, he functioned as chief diplomat. At home he made tours of the West and the South to lead popular opinion to his position in a way that no president had done before him. For the Senate he evidenced a readiness to dispense patronage, woo votes with personal persuasion, and marshal the resources of the political system behind the treaty.

Should McKinley have sought the acquisition of the Philippines? It would be easy to conclude eighty years later that annexation was an error that plunged the nation needlessly into Asian affairs. Yet it is hard to see how the president could have done other than what he did. Forsaking the islands might have meant the reimposition of Spanish rule or, in a more probable scenario, the ascendancy there of Japan or Germany. Whether these powers would have been more humane in subduing Philippine nationalism is at least questionable. To assume that the United States would have turned aside from the Pacific and not become involved there during the twentieth century is attractive but implausible. McKinley made the decisions that best served the national interests.

Later episodes in the administration drew on the wartime precedents. In administering Puerto Rico and Cuba and in suppressing an insurrection in the Philippines, McKinley relied further on the war power, and he shaped affairs from the White House. During the Boxer Rebellion in 1900, he sent troops to China without congressional authorization, governed the new possessions through presidential commissions, and allowed Capitol Hill only a subsidiary role in the process. By 1901 the nation had an empire and a president whose manner and bearing anticipated the imperial executives of six decades later.

William McKinley did not often speculate on his place in history. A man, he once said, might aspire "to be an inspiration for history"; but he would probably not have been surprised that historians have ranked his presidency in the middle range or lower.[23] If the standards of judgment include strength as president and impact on the history of the office, then McKinley's tenure gains in importance. His conduct of the Spanish-American War marked a significant step in the evolution of the modern presidential office and helped to lay the basis for his emergence as the first truly modern president. On his wartime record and on his place as an architect of important departures in American foreign policy rest McKinley's substantial claims as an important figure in the history of the United States.

Notes

CHAPTER 1

1. Charles G. Dawes, *A Journal of the McKinley Years*, ed. Bascom N. Timmons (Chicago: Lakeside Press, 1950), p. 115; George F. Parker, *Recollections of Grover Cleveland* (New York: Century Co., 1909), pp. 249–250.

2. Diary, April 20, 1898, box 52, George B. Cortelyou Papers, Manuscript Division, Library of Congress.

3. Julia B. Foraker, *I Would Live It Again* (New York and London: Harper & Bros., 1932), p. 263.

4. George W. Steevens, *The Land of the Dollar*, 2d ed. (Edinburgh and London: William Blackwood & Sons, 1897), p. 129.

5. Charles S. Olcott, *The Life of William McKinley*, 2 vols. (Boston and New York: Houghton Mifflin Co., 1916), 1:186.

6. Howard Wayne Morgan, *William McKinley and His America* (Syracuse, N.Y.: Syracuse University Press, 1963), pp. 129–134, 142–147.

7. "Reminiscences," Charles Warren Fairbanks Papers, Lilly Library, Indiana University, Bloomington.

8. Olcott, *Life of William McKinley*, 2:346, italics in the original.

9. Statement of Sen. Charles Dick, February 10, 1906, Hanna-McCormick Family Papers, Manuscript Division, Library of Congress.

10. Henry Cabot Lodge to Theodore Roosevelt, December 2, 1896, in *Selections from the Correspondence of Theodore Roosevelt and Henry Cabot Lodge, 1884–1918*, ed. Henry Cabot Lodge, 2 vols. (New York and London: Charles Scribner's Sons, 1925), 1:241.

11. *Public Opinion* 22 (1897): 135.

12. John Sherman to Mark Hanna, November 13, 1896, in Herbert Croly, *Marcus Alonzo Hanna: His Life and Work* (New York: Macmillan Co., 1912), p. 234; Sherman to Hanna, December 15, 1896, William McKinley Papers, Manuscript Division, Library of Congress.

13. McKinley to Sherman, January 4, 1897, and William M. Osborne to Charles Grosvenor, January 6, 1897, McKinley Papers.

14. Sherman to "My Dear Sir," November 8, 1898, in Joseph Benson Foraker, *Notes of a Busy Life*, 2 vols. (Cincinnati, Ohio: Stewart & Kidd Co., 1916), 1:508–509.

15. Osborne to McKinley, December 11, 1896, and McKinley to Joseph Medill, February 8, 1897, McKinley Papers.

16. *New York Times*, December 18, 1895; Henry Cabot Lodge to Theodore Roosevelt, December 2, 1896, in *Selections*, 1:241; Mayo W. Hazeltine, "The Foreign Policy of the New Administration," *North American Review* 164 (1897): 486.

17. Robert M. La Follette, *La Follette's Autobiography* (Madison, Wis.: Robert M. La Follette Co., 1913), p. 115; "La Prorogation de le convention americaine," *L'Exportation française* 25 (1900): 100.

18. Carl Schurz, *Speeches, Correspondence and Political Papers of Carl Schurz*, ed. Frederic Bancroft, 6 vols. (New York: G. P. Putnam's Sons, 1913), 6:270–271.

19. *Speeches and Addresses of William McKinley from March 1,*

1897, to May 30, 1900 (New York: Doubleday & McClure, 1900), p. 24.

20. Lewis L. Gould, *The Presidency of William McKinley* (Lawrence: Regents Press of Kansas, 1980), pp. 40–47.

21. *Speeches and Addresses of William McKinley from May 1, 1897*, pp. 12–13; Morgan, *William McKinley*, p. 297.

22. Charles S. Campbell, Jr., *Anglo-American Understanding, 1898–1903* (Baltimore, Md.: Johns Hopkins Press, 1957), pp. 56–87.

23. William Adam Russ, *The Hawaiian Republic, 1894–98, and Its Struggle to Win Annexation* (Selinsgrove, Pa.: Susquehanna University Press, 1961), p. 127.

24. Merze Tate, *The United States and the Hawaiian Kingdom: A Political History* (New Haven, Conn.: Yale University Press, 1965), pp. 269–271.

25. Ibid., pp. 271–272; William Michael Morgan, "The Anti-Japanese Origins of the Hawaiian Annexation Treaty of 1897," *Diplomatic History* 6 (1982): 23–44.

26. Morgan, "Anti-Japanese Origins," p. 42; U.S., Senate, *Report*, no. 681, 55th Cong., 2d sess. (Washington, D.C.: Government Printing Office, 1898), p. 66.

27. Tate, *United States and the Hawaiian Kingdom*, p. 282; George Frisbie Hoar, *Autobiography of Seventy Years*, 2 vols. (New York: Charles Scribner's Sons, 1903), 2: 308.

28. Henry Cabot Lodge to Stephen P. O'Meara, January 3, 1898, Henry Cabot Lodge Papers, Massachusetts Historical Society, Boston.

29. *Nation* 66 (1898): 80; *New York Times*, March 14, 1898; Diary, June 8, 1898, box 52, Cortelyou Papers.

30. *Pittsburg Times*, March 22, 1897.

31. *Newspaper Maker*, April 1, 1897.

32. Charles Emory Smith, "McKinley in the Cabinet Room," *Saturday Evening Post*, August 30, 1902, p. 1; John Sherman to W. S. Ward, April 28, 1898, John Sherman Papers, Manuscript Division, Library of Congress; Diary, April 16, 1898, box 52, Cortelyou Papers.

33. Thomas C. Platt to Lucien L. Bonheur, January 26, 1898, in author's collection; *New York World*, March 4, 1898.

34. *Canton Repository*, February 9, 1898.

35. *Speeches and Addresses of William McKinley from May 1, 1897*, p. 12.

36. Ibid.

37. George F. W. Holls to Andrew D. White, September 3, 1897, Albert Shaw Papers, in Astor, Lenox and Tilden Foundations, New York Public Library.

CHAPTER 2

1. Philip S. Fomer, *The Spanish-Cuban-American War and the Birth of American Imperialism, 1895–1902*, 2 vols. (New York and London: Monthly Review Press, 1972), 1:2.

2. Ibid., 1:128, 129.

3. Thomas Hart Baker, Jr., "Imperial Finale: Crisis, Decolonization, and War in Spain, 1890–1898" (Ph.D. diss., Princeton University, 1977), pp. 186–187.

4. Ibid., p. 205, quotes the song; Enrique Dupuy de Lôme to Richard Olney, June 4, 1896, U.S., Department of State, *Papers Relating to the Foreign Relations of the United States, 1897* (Washington, D.C.: Government Printing Office, 1898), p. 546 (hereafter cited as *For. Rel.*, with year).

5. *Public Opinion* 23 (1897): 35.

6. Richard Olney to Enrique Dupuy de Lôme, April 4, 1896, *For. Rel.*, 1897, p. 543.

7. Dupuy de Lôme to Olney, June 4, 1896, *For. Rel.*, 1897, p. 547.

8. *A Compilation of the Messages*

and Papers of the Presidents, 1789–1897, comp. James D. Richardson, 10 vols. (Washington, D.C.: Government Printing Office, 1898–1899), 10:719, 721.

9. New York Tribune, April 15, 1897.

10. Foner, Spanish-Cuban-American War, 1:117.

11. John Sherman to Dupuy de Lôme, June 26, 1897, For. Rel., 1897, pp. 507–508.

12. "Offer of Spanish Mission to Mr. Low, May 1897," John Bassett Moore Papers, box 1, Manuscript Division, Library of Congress.

13. Washington Post, October 4, 1897.

14. Sherman to Stewart Woodford, July 16, 1897, For. Rel., 1898, pp. 559–561.

15. Chicago Tribune, November 20, 1897.

16. For. Rel., 1897, p. XX, for McKinley's message.

17. New York Tribune, December 15, 1897; Tasker H. Bliss to Major Wagner, memorandum dated January 3, 1898, Russell A. Alger Papers, William L. Clements Library, University of Michigan, Ann Arbor.

18. Arent S. Crowninshield to John D. Long, February 28, 1898, box 9, William R. Day Papers, Manuscript Division, Library of Congress.

19. Lee to Day, January 12, 1898, For. Rel., 1898, p. 1024; Dupuy de Lôme to Pio Gullon, January 16, 1898, Spanish Diplomatic Correspondence and Documents, 1896–1900: Presented to the Cortes by the Minister of State (Washington, D.C.: Government Printing Office, 1905), pp. 64–65; Baker, "Imperial Finale," p. 310.

20. Julian Pauncefote to Lord Salisbury, January 20, 1898, FO5/2361, Public Record Office, London; U.S., House of Representatives, Congressional Record, 55th Cong., 2d sess. (January 19, 1898), p. 769.

21. Memorandum of Day's interview with Dupuy de Lôme, January 24,

1898, box 35, Day Papers.

22. Memorandum, January 24, 1898, box 35, Day Papers; Lee to Day, January 26, 1898, box 124, Moore Papers; Dupuy de Lôme to Pio Gullon, January 28, 1898, Spanish Diplomatic Correspondence, p. 71.

23. Woodford to Gullon, December 20, 1897, and Gullon to Woodford, February 1, 1898, For. Rel., 1898, pp. 649, 664, 660.

24. Dupuy de Lôme to Don José Canalejas, n.d., For. Rel., 1898, pp. 1007–1008.

25. Lee to Day, February 16, 1898, For. Rel., 1898, p. 1029; D. W. Dickens, "Memorandum for the Secretary," December 8, 1898, Ohio State Historical Society, Columbus.

26. John L. Offner, "President McKinley and the Origins of the Spanish-American War" (Ph.D. diss., Pennsylvania State University, 1957), p. 213; Speeches and Addresses of William McKinley from March 1, 1897, to May 30, 1900 (New York: Doubleday & McClure, 1900), p. 77.

27. Offner, "President McKinley," p. 221; Ernest R. May, Imperial Democracy: The Emergence of America as a Great Power (New York: Harcourt, Brace & World, 1961), pp. 142, 143.

28. New York Tribune, March 8, 1898; Theodore Roosevelt to John D. Long, February 16, 1898, in The Letters of Theodore Roosevelt, ed. Elting E. Morison et al., 8 vols. (Cambridge, Mass.: Harvard University Press, 1951–1954), 1:773.

29. Woodford to McKinley, March 8, 1898, For. Rel., 1898, p. 684.

30. "Memoranda prepared by H[oratio]. S. R[ubens]. and delivered to Assistant Secretary Day, March 1, 1898," box 56, Cortelyou Papers; Foner, Spanish-Cuban-American War, 1:248.

31. Diary, March 19, 1898, Oscar S. Straus Papers, Manuscript Division, Library of Congress.

32. Woodford to McKinley, March 19, 1898, *For. Rel.*, 1898, p. 693, italics in original.

33. *Congressional Record*, 55th Cong., 2d sess. (March 17, 1898), pp. 2919, 2917; Francis E. Warren to Gibson Clark, Francis E. Warren Papers, University of Wyoming Library, Laramie.

34. John Coit Spooner to N. L. James, March 14, 1898, John Coit Spooner Papers, Manuscript Division, Library of Congress; *Nation* 66 (1898): 195; Paul S. Holbo, "The Convergence of Moods and the Cuban-Bond 'Conspiracy' of 1898," *Journal of American History* 55 (1968): 59.

35. Diary, March 26, 1898, box 52, Cortelyou Papers; *New York Tribune*, April 1, 1898; Hermann Hagedorn, *Leonard Wood*, 2 vols. (New York: Harper & Bros., 1931), 1:141; John Davis Long, *America of Yesterday, as Reflected in the Journal of John Davis Long*, ed. Lawrence Shaw Mayo (Boston: Atlantic Monthly Press, 1923), p. 175.

36. Day to Woodford, March 20, 1898, *For Rel.*, 1898, pp. 692–693; *New York Herald*, March 25, 1898.

37. Day to Woodford, March 26 and 28, 1898, and Woodford to Day, March 27, 1898, *For. Rel.*, 1898, pp. 704, 712–713.

38. Day to Woodford, March 27, 1898, *For. Rel.*, 1898, pp. 711–712.

39. Woodford to Day, March 31, 1898, *For. Rel.*, 1898, pp. 726–727.

40. *New York Herald*, March 29, 1898; Diary, March 29, 1898, box 52, Cortelyou Papers; *Congressional Record*, 55th Cong., 2d sess. (March 28, 1898), pp. 3278–3279.

41. *New York Tribune*, April 2, 1898; Diary, March 31, 1898, box 52, Cortelyou Papers; Elihu Root to Cornelius N. Bliss, April 2, 1898, Elihu Root Papers, Manuscript Division, Library of Congress.

42. Woodford to McKinley, April 3, 1898, and Day to Woodford, April 3 and 4, 1898, *For. Rel.*, 1898, pp. 732–733.

43. Lee to Day, April 6, 1898, quoted in Offner, "President McKinley," p. 328; Diary, April 6, 1898, box 52, Cortelyou Papers; Journal, April 6, 1898, Lodge Papers.

44. *For. Rel.*, 1898, pp. 740–741.

45. Baker, "Imperial Finale," p. 392.

46. Woodford to McKinley, April 10, 1898, Luis Polo de Bernabé to John Sherman, April 10, 1898, *For. Rel.*, 1898, pp. 747–748; May, *Imperial Democracy*, p. 157.

47. Baker, "Imperial Finale," p. 394.

48. Journal, April 4, 1898, John D. Long Papers, Massachusetts Historical Society, Boston.

49. *For. Rel.*, 1898, pp. 754–755; Henry Cabot Lodge, *The War with Spain* (New York and London: Harper & Bros., 1899), p. 35.

50. *For. Rel.*, 1898, pp. 757–759; Lodge, *War with Spain*, p. 35.

51. *For. Rel.*, 1898, pp. 759, 760.

52. *Washington Star*, April 11, 1898; Diary, April 12, 1898, box 52, Cortelyou Papers.

53. *Washington Star*, April 14, 1898; *Washington Evening Times*, April 11, 1898, quoted in Paul S. Holbo, "Presidential Leadership in Foreign Affairs: William McKinley and the Turpie-Foraker Amendment," *American Historical Review* 72 (1967): 1325; *Congressional Record*, 55th Cong., 2d sess. (April 13, 1898), pp. 3819–3820.

54. Holbo, "Presidential Leadership," p. 1328; William Boyd Allison to M. M. Ham, April 18, 1898, William Boyd Allison Papers, box 323, Iowa State Department of History and Archives, Des Moines.

55. *Washington Star*, April 16, 1898; Cornelius N. Bliss to Root, April 19, 1898, Root Papers; Holbo, "Presidential Leadership," p. 1333.

56. Walter LaFeber, *The New Em-*

pire: *An Interpretation of American Expansion, 1860–1898* (Ith-

aca, N.Y.: Cornell University Press, 1963), p. 400.

CHAPTER 3

1. Redfield Proctor to Russell A. Alger, August 15, 1898, Alger Papers.

2. Diary, June 8, 1898, box 52, Cortelyou Papers; Charles Emory Smith to Elihu Root, August 12, 1903, Henry C. Corbin Papers, Manuscript Division, Library of Congress.

3. Adolphus W. Greely, *Reminiscences of Adventure and Service: A Record of Sixty-five Years* (New York and London: Charles Scribner's Sons, 1927), p. 179.

4. Richard T. Loomis, "The White House Telephone and Crisis Management," *United States Naval Institute Proceedings* 45 (1969): 64–65.

5. Henry S. Pritchett, "Some Recollections of President McKinley and the Cuban Intervention," *North American Review* 189 (1909): 399; De B. Randolph Keim, "The President's War," *Frank Leslie's Popular Monthly* 50 (1900): 120, 121.

6. Cushman K. Davis to C. A. Severance, May 5, 1898, Cushman K. Davis Papers, Minnesota Historical Society, St. Paul.

7. Theodore Roosevelt to George Dewey, February 25, 1898, in *The Letters of Theodore Roosevelt*, ed. Elting E. Morison et al., 8 vols. (Cambridge, Mass.: Harvard University Press, 1951–1954), 1:784–785.

8. John A. S. Grenville, "American Naval Preparations for War with Spain, 1896–1898," *Journal of American Studies* 2 (1968): 43.

9. Long to Agnes Long, October 9, 1898, Long Papers; Long to Dewey, April 24, 1898, in John Davis Long, *The New American Navy*, 2 vols. (New York: Outlook Co., 1903), 1:181–182.

10. Memorandum read by William R.

Day to Sir Julian Pauncefote, March 16, 1898, box 8, Day Papers; Thomas J. McCormick, *China Market: America's Quest for Informal Empire, 1893–1901* (Chicago: Quadrangle Books, 1967), pp. 96, 97, 99–100.

11. McKinley to Alger, May 4, 1898, U.S., Army, *Correspondence Relating to the War with Spain and Conditions Growing out of the Same, Including the Insurrection in the Philippine Islands and the China Relief Expedition, between the Adjutant-General of the Army and Military Commanders in the United States, Cuba, Porto Rico, China, and the Philippine Islands, from April 15, 1898, to July 30, 1902*, 2 vols. (Washington, D.C.: Government Printing Office, 1902), 2:635 (hereafter cited as *Correspondence*); Memorandum, May 9, 1898, box 186, and undated memorandum, box 192, Moore Papers.

12. Theodore Schwan to Wesley Merritt, May 16, 1898, and McKinley to Alger, May 19, 1898, *Correspondence*, 2:649, 676, 677; *New York Tribune*, June 2, 1898.

13. Hay to Day, May 3, 1898, John Hay Papers, Manuscript Division, Library of Congress; *New York Tribune*, May 6 and 27 and June 4, 1898; William P. Frye to James H. Wilson, June 6, 1898, Wilson Papers.

14. Henry Cabot Lodge to William Laffan, June 16, 1898, Lodge Papers.

15. Undated memorandum, box 192, Moore Papers; Day to Hay, June 3, 1898, Hay Papers.

16. E. Spencer Pratt to Day, April 28, 1898, and *Singapore Free Press*, June 1, 1898, enclosed with Pratt to Day, June 2, 1898, in *A Treaty of Peace between the United States*

and Spain: *Message from the President of the United States, Transmitting a Treaty of Peace between the United States and Spain, Signed at the City of Paris, on December 10, 1898,* Senate document no. 62, 55th Cong., 3d sess. (Washington, D.C.: Government Printing Office, 1899), pp. 321, 342, 347 (hereafter cited as *Treaty of Peace*).

17. United States, Senate, *Communiciations between the Executive Departments of the Government and Aguinaldo,* Senate document no. 208, 56th Cong., 1st sess., pp. 88, 89; Long to Dewey, May 26, 1898, in Long, *New American Navy* 2:109; Pratt to Day, April 28, 1898, *Treaty of Peace,* p. 342; Long to Alger, May 27, 1898, *Correspondence,* 2:674.

18. Day to Hay, June 14, 1898, Hay Papers; Long to Dewey, June 14, 1898, box 186, Moore Papers.

19. Day to Pratt, June 16, 1898 (wire and letter), and July 20, 1898, *Treaty of Peace,* pp. 353–354, 357.

20. Charles S. Olcott, *The Life of William McKinley,* 2 vols. (Boston and New York: Houghton Mifflin Co., 1916), 2:165; Journal, July 7, 1898, William Laffan to Lodge, July 14, 1898, Lodge Papers.

21. Charles Emory Smith to Root, August 12, 1903, Corbin Papers.

22. Diary, May 15, 1898, box 52, Cortelyou Papers; Francis E. Warren to F. E. Wolcott, May 28, 1898, Warren Papers.

23. "Charges of Incompetence in the Army," *Literary Digest* 16 (1898): 722.

24. *Speeches and Addresses of William McKinley from March 1, 1897, to May 30, 1900* (New York: Doubleday & McClure, 1900), p. 187.

25. Tomas Estrada Palma to McKinley, April 26, 1898, box 68, Cortelyou Papers.

26. Long, *New American Navy,* 1: 238; Roosevelt to Lodge, June 10,

1898, in *Letters of Theodore Roosevelt,* 2:837; Shafter to Corbin, June 7, 1898, Corbin Papers.

27. Corbin to Shafter, May 30, 1898 (sent on May 31), *Correspondence,* 1:18–19.

28. Corbin to Shafter, June 1, 1898, and Alger to Shafter, June 7, 1898, *Correspondence,* 1:21, 30; Shafter to Corbin, June 7, 1898, Corbin Papers; Roosevelt to Lodge, June 12, 1898, in *Letters of Theodore Roosevelt,* 2:841.

29. Shafter to Alger, July 1, 1898, Shafter to Corbin, July 1 and 2, 1898, Shafter to Alger, July 3, 1898, Alger to Shafter, July 3, 1898, and Corbin to Shafter, July 3, 1898, *Correspondence,* 1:70, 72, 74–75, 76.

30. Corbin to Shafter, July 4, 1898, *Correspondence,* 1:82.

31. Draft of Corbin to Shafter, July 9, 1898, with McKinley's changes, box 68, Cortelyou Papers; Corbin to Shafter, July 9, 1898, *Correspondence,* 1:119; Olcott, *Life of William McKinley,* 2:50.

32. Miles to Alger, July 13, 1898, *Correspondence,* 1:134.

33. John Davis Long, *America of Yesterday, as Reflected in the Journal of John Davis Long,* ed. Lawrence Shaw Mayo (Boston: Atlantic Monthly Press, 1923), pp. 203–204; Alger to Miles, July 13, 1898, and Corbin to Shafter, July 13, 1898, *Correspondence,* 1:135–136.

34. Jules Patenôtre to Théophile Delcassé, July 9, 1898, and Delcassé to Jules Cambon, July 19, 1898, Ministere des Affaires étrangères, *Documents diplomatiques français, 1871–1914,* vol. 14: *4 janvier–30 décembre 1898* (Paris: Costes, 1957), pp. 376, 393.

35. "Autobiography," box 213, Moore Papers; Cambon to Delcassé, July 8, 1898, *Documents diplomatiques français,* p. 372.

36. Cambon to Delcassé, July 27, 1898, *Documents diplomatiques français,* p. 403; Diary, July 26, 1898, box 52, Cortelyou Papers; James Wilson to William Boyd

Allison, August 3, 1898, box 329, Allison Papers.

37. Hay to Day, July 14, 1898, in Alfred L. P. Dennis, *Adventures in American Diplomacy, 1896–1906* (New York: E. P. Dutton & Co., 1928), p. 93.

38. Dewey to Long, July 4, 1898, quoted in Ronald Spector, *Admiral of the New Empire: The Life and Career of George Dewey* (Baton Rouge: Louisiana State University Press, 1974), p. 81; Andrew D. White to Day, July 12 and 13, 1898, and Day to White, July 14, 1898, Dispatches from Germany, State Department, record group 59, National Archives.

39. Aguinaldo to McKinley, June 10, 1898, *Treaty of Peace*, pp. 360–361; Dewey to Long, June 27, 1898, in *Annual Reports of the Navy Department for the Year 1898, Appendix to the Report of the Chief of the Bureau of Navigation*, House document no. 3, vol. 12, 55th Cong., 3d sess. (Washington, D.C.: Government Printing Office, 1898), p. 103.

40. "Relations of U.S. to Philippine Insurgents," July 20, 1898, box 187, Moore Papers.

41. Cambon to Hanotaux, June 24, 1898, *Documents diplomatiques français*, p. 357, quotes Cleveland; Joseph B. Foraker to W. S. Cappeller, July 29, 1898, Joseph B. Foraker Papers, Cincinnati Historical Society; Lodge to Day, July 29, 1898, box 10, Day Papers; McCormick, *China Market*, p. 115.

42. McKinley Memorandum, July 26, 1898, McKinley Papers.

43. Wilson to Allison, August 3, 1898, box 329, Allison Papers; Merritt to Corbin, August 1, 1898, *Correspondence*, 2:743; Dewey to Long, July 26, 1898, *Annual Reports of the Navy Department for the Year 1898, Appendix*, p. 118.

44. Olcott, *Life of William McKinley*, 2:63; Diary, July 30 and 31, 1898, box 52, Cortelyou Papers.

45. Cambon to Delcassé, July 31, 1898, *Documents diplomatiques français*, pp. 409–413; Diary, July 30, 1898, box 52, Cortelyou Papers.

46. Almodóvar del Rio to León y Castillo, August 1, 1898, and León y Castillo to Almodóvar del Rio, August 4, 1898, *Spanish Diplomatic Correspondence and Documents, 1896–1900: Presented to the Cortes by the Minister of State* (Washington, D.C.: Government Printing Office, 1905), pp. 214–217.

47. Shafter to Corbin, August 2, 1898, and Alger to Shafter, August 2, 1898, *Correspondence*, 1:194, 196.

48. Shafter to Corbin, August 3, 1898, and Alger to Shafter, August 4, 1898, *Correspondence*, 1:200, 204.

49. Shafter to Corbin, August 3, 1898, *Correspondence*, 1:202; Roosevelt to Shafter, August 3, 1898, in *Letters of Theodore Roosevelt*, 2:864–865.

50. McKinley to Shafter, August 5, 1898, draft in box 56, Diary, August 4, 1898, box 52, Cortelyou Papers.

51. León y Castillo to Almodóvar del Rio, August 11, 1898, *Spanish Diplomatic Correspondence*, pp. 219–220; Cambon to Delcassé, August 10, 1898, *Documents diplomatiques français*, pp. 444–445.

52. *Spectator*, July 30, 1898, clipping enclosed with Hay to McKinley, August 2, 1898, box 56, and Diary, July 30, 1898, box 52, Cortelyou Papers.

53. Draft of letter, McKinley to Commission for the Evacuation of Cuba, December 6, 1898, with Cortelyou's note of McKinley's remark, box 70, "Suggestions, Protocol, August 12, 1898," box 56, Cortelyou Papers.

CHAPTER 4

1. F. H. Gillette to John D. Long, August 5, 1898, Long Papers; George Fred Williams to Moreton Frewen, September 21, 1898, Moreton Frewen Papers, Manuscript Division, Library of Congress.
2. "The Bombardment of the War Department," *Literary Digest* 17 (1898): 303.
3. *New York Tribune*, September 4, 1898.
4. Diary, August 23, 1898, box 52, Cortelyou Papers.
5. James Wilson to McKinley, September 7, 1898, box 69, Cortelyou Papers; Alger to McKinley, September 8, 1898, in Russell A. Alger, *The Spanish-American War* (New York and London: Harper & Bros., 1901), p. 376.
6. *Speeches and Addresses of William McKinley from March 1, 1897, to May 30, 1900* (New York: Doubleday & McClure, 1900), p. 82.
7. Frank L. Brown to Joseph L. Bristow, April 27, 1898, Joseph L. Bristow Papers, Kansas State Historical Society, Topeka; *New York Tribune*, August 25, 1898.
8. Joseph W. Babcock to Jacob H. Gallinger, August 27, 1898, Jacob H. Gallinger Papers, New Hampshire Historical Society, Concord; *New York Tribune*, August 31, 1898; William P. Hepburn to John F. Lacey, September 12, 1898, John F. Lacey Papers, Iowa State Department of History and Archives, Des Moines.
9. Henry W. Lawton to Henry C. Corbin, August 16, 1898, and Corbin to Lawton, August 16, 1898, U.S., Army, *Correspondence Relating to the War with Spain . . .* , 2 vols. (Washington, D.C.: Government Printing Office, 1902), 1:230, 231 (hereafter cited as *Correspondence*).
10. David F. Healy, *The United States in Cuba, 1898–1902: Generals, Politicians, and the Search for Policy* (Madison: University of Wisconsin Press, 1963), pp. 50, 51.
11. Tyler Dennett, *John Hay: From Poetry to Politics* (New York: Dodd, Mead, & Co., 1933), p. 197.
12. William P. Frye to William E. Chandler, September 6, 1898, William E. Chandler Papers, New Hampshire Historical Society, Concord.
13. Chandler to McKinley, August 17, 1898, McKinley Papers.
14. Wesley Merritt and George Dewey to Corbin, August 13, 1898, and Corbin to Merritt, August 17, 1898, *Correspondence*, 2:754.
15. Merritt to Corbin, received August 27, 1898, and Corbin to E. S. Otis, September 7, 1898, *Correspondence*, 2:765, 788.
16. Otis to Emilio Aguinaldo, September 8, 1898, and Otis to Corbin, September 16, 1898, *Correspondence*, 2:826, 791.
17. Memorandums, August 4, 1898, and September 8, 1898, box 187, Moore Papers.
18. Pierre J. Smith to McKinley, September 15, 1898, box 68, Cortelyou Papers; George F. W. Holls to Andrew D. White, September 10, 1898, Albert Shaw Papers; *New York Tribune*, September 15, 1898.
19. U.S., Department of State, *Papers Relating to the Foreign Relations of the United States*, 1898 (Washington, D.C.: Government Printing Office, 1901), pp. 904-908, for McKinley's instructions (hereafter cited as *For. Rel.*, with year).
20. George McAneny to Carl Schurz, September 17, 1898, Carl Schurz Papers, Manuscript Division, Library of Congress.
21. McKinley to Garret A. Hobart, September 19, 1898, McKinley Papers; "Memoranda Concerning the Situation in the Philippines on August 30, 1898, by F. V. Greene, Major General, Volunteers, and Accompanying Papers," *Treaty of Peace*, pp. 422, 424, 425.

22. Memorandum, October 1, 1898, Felipe Agoncillo, "Memorandum," October 4, 1898, and Hay to Day, October 4, 1898, McKinley Papers.

23. Charles Emory Smith, "McKinley in the Cabinet Room," *Saturday Evening Post*, October 11, 1902, p. 7; *Speeches and Addresses of William McKinley from March 1, 1897*, pp. 87, 90–91, 105, 114.

24. *Speeches and Addresses of William McKinley from May 1, 1897*, pp. 98, 117, 131, 153.

25. Ibid., p. 137.

26. Joseph W. Babcock to John Coit Spooner, October 15, 1898, Spooner Papers; *New York Tribune*, October 22, 1898.

27. Hay to McKinley, November 9, 1898, box 57, Cortelyou Papers.

28. Day to McKinley, September 30, 1898, McKinley Papers; Whitelaw Reid, *Making Peace with Spain: The Diary of Whitelaw Reid, September–December 1898*, ed. H. Wayne Morgan (Austin: University of Texas Press, 1965), p. 53.

29. Hay to Day, October 13, 1898, Day to Hay, October 22, 1898, and Hay to Day, October 23, 1898, *For. Rel.*, 1898, pp. 927–930.

30. Reid, *Making Peace with Spain*, pp. 104, 112, 113; Day to Hay, October 25, 1898, *For. Rel.*, 1898, p. 931.

31. Reid, *Making Peace with Spain*, pp. 114–117; Day to Alvey Adee, October 27, 1898, *For. Rel.*, 1898, pp. 936–937.

32. Reid, *Making Peace with Spain*, p. 82; Hay to Day, October 14, 1898, *For. Rel.*, 1898, p. 928.

33. Peace Commissioners to Hay, October 25, 1898, *For. Rel.*, 1898, pp. 932–935.

34. Hay to Day, October 28, 1898, *For. Rel.*, 1898, pp. 937–938. There is a draft of this message in McKinley's handwriting, box 69, Cortelyou Papers.

35. Charles S. Olcott, *The Life of William McKinley*, 2 vols. (Boston and New York: Houghton Mifflin Co., 1916), 2:109–111.

36. James F. Rusling, *Men and Things I Saw in Civil War Days* (New York: Eaton & Mains, 1899), p. 15; McKinley used a variant of this Lincoln story himself in 1892. *Speeches and Addresses of William McKinley from His Election to Congress to the Present Time* (New York: D. Appleton & Co., 1893), p. 607.

37. *Washington Post*, November 24, 1899.

38. Frye to Adee, October 30, 1898, and Hay to Frye, November 1, 1898, *For. Rel.*, 1898, pp. 939–940.

39. *Speeches and Addresses of William McKinley from May 1, 1897*, pp. 158, 161, 174, 182; *New York Tribune*, December 16, 1898; Asher Hinds Diary, December 19, 1898, Manuscript Division, Library of Congress.

40. U.S., Senate, *Congressional Record*, 55th Cong., 3d sess. (January 24, 1899), p. 959.

41. *New York Tribune*, December 14, 1898.

42. Lodge to Paul Dana, January 26, 1899, Lodge Papers; Hoar to Schurz, January 28, 1899, Schurz Papers; Charles W. Fairbanks to W. T. Durbin, February 1, 1899, Fairbanks Papers.

43. Diary, February 4, 1899, box 52, Cortelyou Papers.

44. Otis to Alger, received October 30, 1898, and Otis to Corbin, November 13, 1898, *Correspondence*, 2:831, 836.

45. Corbin to Otis, December 4, 1898, *Correspondence*, 2:850.

46. Corbin to Otis, December 21, 1898, *Correspondence*, 2:857.

47. McKinley to Alger, December 21, 1898, *Correspondence*, 2:858–859.

48. Alger to Otis, December 29 and 30, 1898, and Otis to Alger, December 30, 1898, *Correspondence*, 2:863, 864.

49. Corbin to Otis, January 8, 1899, *Correspondence*, 2:872–873.

50. Jacob Gould Schurman, *Philippine Affairs* (New York: Charles Scribner's Sons, 1902), pp. 1–2.
51. Dewey to Long, received February 5, 1899, *Correspondence*, 2: 893.
52. *Speeches and Addresses of William McKinley from May 1, 1897,* pp. 187, 188, 189, 191, 192, 193.

CHAPTER 5

1. W. M. Osborne to McKinley, March 3, 1899, McKinley Papers.
2. Graham A. Cosmas, *An Army for Empire: The United States Army in the Spanish-American War* (Columbia: University of Missouri Press, 1971), pp. 295–296.
3. Albert Shaw to George F. W. Holls, July 21, 1899, Shaw Papers; Philip C. Jessup, *Elihu Root*, 2 vols. (New York: Dodd, Mead & Co., 1938), 1:215–216.
4. Dean C. Worcester, *The Philippines, Past and Present* (New York: Macmillan Co., 1930), p. 790; John Hay to J. G. Schurman, May 5, 1899, U.S., Senate, *Communications between the Executive Departments of the Government and Aguinaldo, Etc.,* Senate document no. 208, 56th Cong., 1st sess., p. 156.
5. *Report of the (Schurman) Philippine Commission to the President,* Senate document no. 138, 56th Cong., 1st sess., 4 vols. (Washington, D.C.: Government Printing Office, 1900–1901), 1:175; Charles S. Olcott, *The Life of William McKinley*, 2 vols. (Boston and New York: Houghton Mifflin Co., 1916), 2:175.
6. *Speeches and Addresses of William McKinley from March 1, 1897, to May 30, 1900* (New York: Doubleday & McClure, 1900), pp. 213, 216.
7. The recent charges of genocide arose from the repeated but erroneous assertions of Gore Vidal, based on a mistaken quotation, that three million Filipinos had been killed. The figure in the original source, three hundred thousand Filipinos, was also probably inflated. For the revelation of Vidal's mistake by John M. Gates and the subsequent controversy, see *New York Review of Books,* December 17, 1981, and March 4, 1982.
8. *Official Proceedings of the Twelfth Republican National Convention . . . 1900,* reported by Milton W. Blumenberg (Philadelphia: Press of Dunlap Printing Co., 1900), pp. 175, 178.
9. Hermann Hagedorn, *Leonard Wood: A Biography,* 2 vols. (New York and London: Harper & Bros., 1931), 1:261; *Annual Report of the War Department for the Fiscal Year Ended June 30, 1899, Report of the Secretary of War,* House document no. 2, 56th Cong., 1st sess. (Washington, D.C.: Government Printing Office, 1899), pp. 31–32; *A Supplement to A Compilation of the Messages and Papers of the Presidents, 1789–1902, by James D. Richardson,* comp. George Raywood Devitt (Washington, D.C.: Bureau of National Literature and Art, 1903), pp. 74–75.
10. Hagedorn, *Leonard Wood,* 1:266.
11. Root to Leonard Wood, February 9, 1901, McKinley Papers; Jessup, *Elihu Root,* 1:310–311; *New York Tribune,* February 2, 1901; David F. Healy, *The United States in Cuba, 1898–1902: Generals, Politicians, and the Search for Policy* (Madison: University of Wisconsin Press, 1963), pp. 150–167.
12. Memorandum, March 15, 1916, box 76, Cortelyou Papers, quotes McKinley; Root to Wood, February 9, 1901, McKinley Papers.
13. Philip S. Foner, *The Spanish-Cuban-American War and the Birth of American Imperialism,*

1895–1902, 2 vols. (New York: Monthly Review Press, 1972), 2: 593.

14. Root to Wood, April 2, 1901, McKinley Papers.

15. *Supplement to A Compilation of the Messages and Papers,* p. 100.

16. *New York Tribune,* January 29, 1900; Charles G. Dawes, *A Journal of the McKinley Years,* ed. Bascom N. Timmons (Chicago: Lakeside Press, 1950), p. 217.

17. *Papers Relating to the Foreign Relations of the United States,* 1898, House document no. 1, 55th Cong., 3d sess. (Washington, D.C.: Government Printing Office, 1901), p. 907.

18. *Papers Relating to the Foreign Relations of the United States,*

1901, *Appendix: Affairs in China,* p. 12.

19. "Talk with John Hay," July 1, 1900, box 214, John Bassett Moore Papers, Library of Congress; McKinley to Hay, September 14, 1900, Hay Papers.

20. Olcott, *Life of William McKinley,* 2:379, 382, 384.

21. John Hay, *Addresses of John Hay* (New York: Century Co., 1906), p. 175.

22. David F. Trask, *The War with Spain in 1898* (New York: Macmillan Publishing Co., 1981), p. 484.

23. Margaret Leech, *In the Days of McKinley* (New York: Harper & Bros., 1959), p. vi.

Bibliographical Essay

The basic manuscript source for a study of William McKinley and the Spanish-American War is the microfilm edition of his papers that are housed in the Manuscripts Division of the Library of Congress (hereafter LC). The ninety-eight reels contain the incoming correspondence, the president's letter books, the outgoing letters of his secretaries, and clippings, speeches, and other data. Rivaling the McKinley Papers in importance are the papers of his secretary, George B. Cortelyou. Cortelyou took custody of the president's records after McKinley died, and he gave part of them to the Library of Congress in 1935. Some part of the collection remained with the Cortelyou family, because an addition to the Cortelyou Papers (LC) contributed the secretary's diaries and some twenty boxes of McKinley materials. The boxes on the Spanish-American War are especially rich with cables, memoranda, and draft documents that illuminate how decisions were made.

The papers of the cabinet officers are also useful for understanding the conflict. The William Rufus Day Papers (LC) are central for the coming of the war with Spain and the peace-making process. The Russell A. Alger Papers, William L. Clements Library, University of Michigan, outline what the secretary did during the war and how he tried to defend himself when his tenure became controversial. The John D. Long Papers, Massachusetts Historical Society, Boston, are most useful for Long's own journal. The John Hay Papers (LC) and the Elihu Root Papers (LC) disclose the activities of the two cabinet officials that oversaw the postwar diplomatic and military consequences of the war. Among the records of subcabinet officials, the John Bassett Moore Papers (LC) contain significant documents about the war and the peace negotiations.

In the National Archives, the State Department files, record group 59, Dispatches from United States Ministers to Spain, 1897/1898, were central to evaluating Stewart Woodford's part in the coming of the war. The Records of the Department of State Relating to the Paris Peace Commission, 1898, RG 43, contain little that is not in the 1898 volume of *Foreign Relations*.

For the war with Spain, the following collections of private papers were useful: William E. Chandler Papers (LC); the Henry

Cabot Lodge Papers, Massachusetts Historical Society, Boston; the Whitelaw Reid Papers (LC); the Carl Schurz Papers (LC); the Albert Shaw Papers, New York Public Library; the Oscar Straus Papers (LC); and the James H. Wilson Papers (LC).

Because the Spanish-American War produced continuing controversies, the documentary collections in print in McKinley's presidency are unusually important. Simply reading these materials will provide important insights into how the war affected the nation. *Speeches and Addresses of William McKinley from March 1, 1897, to May 30, 1900* (New York: Doubleday & McClure, 1900) is an extremely revealing compilation. It shows how McKinley used rhetoric to shape and move opinion. Volume 10 of *A Compilation of the Messages and Papers of the Presidents, 1789–1897*, comp. James D. Richardson, 10 vols. (Washington, D.C.: Government Printing Office, 1899), contains data on McKinley. Most pertinent for this study was *A Supplement to A Compilation of the Messages and Papers of the President, 1789–1902, by James D. Richardson*, comp. George Raywood Devitt (Washington, D.C.: Bureau of National Literature and Art, 1903).

For McKinley's foreign policies, *Papers Relating to the Foreign Relations of the United States, 1897–1901* (Washington, D.C.: Government Printing Office, 1897–1902), were indispensable. The 1898 volume contains important information on the advent of the Spanish-American War and the peace negotiations. United States Congress, Senate, *A Treaty of Peace between the United States and Spain*, 55th Cong., 3d sess., Senate document no. 2 (Washington, D.C.: Government Printing Office 1898), has an abundance of data on the administration's actions toward the Philippines in 1898.

On the war with Spain, the fighting in the Philippines, and the Boxer Rebellion, many significant documents can be found in *Correspondence Relating to the War with Spain and Conditions Growing out of the Same, Including Insurrection in the Philippine Islands and the China Relief Expedition, between the Adjutant-General of the Army and Military Commanders in the United States, Cuba, Porto Rico, China, and the Philippine Islands from April 15, 1898 to July 30, 1902*, 2 vols. (Washington, D.C.: Government Printing Office, 1902). The two investigations of the War Department and the army in 1898 and 1899 have relevant data. See, United States Congress, Senate, *Report of the Commission Appointed by the President to Investigate the Conduct of the War Department in the War with Spain*, 56th Cong., 1st sess., Senate document no. 221, 8 vols. (Washington, D.C.: Government Printing Office, 1900), and United States Congress, Senate, *Food Furnished by the Subsistence Department to Troops in the Field,* 56th Cong., 1st sess., Senate document no. 270, 3 vols. (Washington, D.C.: Government Printing Office, 1900).

For the diplomacy of the Spanish war, the volume of *Spanish Diplomatic Correspondence and Documents, 1896–1900: Presented to the Cortes by the Minister of State* (Washington, D.C.: Government Printing Office, 1905) was central. Ministère des Affaires étrangères, *Documents diplomatiques français, 1871–1914,* vol. 14: *4 janvier–30 decembre 1898* (Paris: Costes, 1957), prints the important documents of the French intermediaries during the summer of 1898.

The newspapers of the late nineteenth century provide a wealth of information. Careful reading often reveals subtle shifts in government policy, and the premeditated news leak was as common then as it is in contemporary Washington. The *New York Tribune* covered the White House from a Republican perspective. The *Washington Star* was equally enlightening. The *New York Times* was not yet the excellent newspaper it became in the mid twentieth century. The same can be said of the *Washington Post.* The *Literary Digest* and *Public Opinion* provide a weekly running account of press views and editorial opinion. The journals and periodicals of·the day are vital. The *Forum, Nation, North American Review,* and *American Monthly Review of Reviews* are the most rewarding for foreign-policy developments.

Aside from campaign biographies and books written soon after the president's death, the first serious biography of McKinley was Charles S. Olcott's *Life of William McKinley,* 2 vols. (Boston and New York: Houghton Mifflin Co., 1916). The McKinley Papers and the Cortelyou Papers were Olcott's major sources, and his insights have now largely been superseded. Margaret Leech's *In the Days of McKinley* (New York: Harper & Bros., 1959) covers the presidency in great detail. Leech had the Cortelyou diary, as well as McKinley's papers, at her disposal, and her portrait of her subject is detailed and in many places persuasive. Howard Wayne Morgan's *William McKinley and His America* (Syracuse, N.Y.: Syracuse University Press, 1963) is a full life that reflects Morgan's mastery of the politics of the Gilded Age. His conclusions about McKinley are more cautious than is the evidence of presidential strength that he offers. Briefer assessments of McKinley's career are H. Wayne Morgan's "William McKinley as a Political Leader," *Review of Politics* 28 (1966): 417–432; Lewis L. Gould's "William

McKinley and the Expansion of Presidential Power," *Ohio History* 87 (1978): 5–20; and Richard H. Bradford's unpublished essay "Mask in the Pageant: William McKinley and American Historians."

Among the memoirs and letters of men around McKinley, the following bear most directly on the conflict with Spain. Russell A. Alger, in *The Spanish-American War* (New York and London: Harper & Bros., 1901), offers a lengthy and somewhat labored defense of his cabinet career. For John D. Long, see his article "Some Personal Characteristics of President McKinley," *Century Magazine* 63 (1901): 144–146, and his book *The New American Navy*, 2 vols. (New York: Outlook Co., 1903). *America of Yesterday, as Reflected in the Journal of John Davis Long*, ed. Lawrence Shaw Mayo (Boston: Atlantic Monthly Press, 1923), has the best segments of Long's account of his cabinet service. *Papers of John Davis Long, 1897–1904*, ed. Gardner Weld Allen (Boston: Massachusetts Historical Society, 1939), reprints the most relevant letters that Long received. Henry S. Pritchett, "Some Recollections of President McKinley and the Cuban Intervention," *North American Review* 189 (1909): 397–403, is illuminating. Adolphus W. Greeley's *Reminiscences of Adventure and Service: A Record of Sixty-five Years* (New York and London: Charles Scribner's Sons, 1927) has an interesting chapter on wartime communications of the White House. The first two volumes of *The Letters of Theodore Roosevelt*, ed. Elting Morison et al., 8 vols. (Cambridge, Mass.: Harvard University Press, 1951–1954), have most of Roosevelt's communications to or about McKinley. See also Lewis L. Gould, ed., "Theodore Roosevelt and the Spanish-American War: Four Unpublished Letters to President William McKinley," *Theodore Roosevelt Association Journal* 7 (1981): 17–21. *Letters and Papers of Alfred Thayer Mahan*, ed. Robert Seager II and Doris D. Maguire, 3 vols. (Annapolis, Md.: Naval Institute Press, 1975), is useful for the navy's role in the war.

Biographical treatments of McKinley's associates in the war include George William Duncan's "The Diplomatic Career of William Rufus Day, 1897–1898" (Ph.D. dissertation, Case Western Reserve University, 1976), a thorough study; Ronald Spector's *Admiral of the New Empire: The Life and Career of George Dewey* (Baton Rouge: Louisiana State University Press, 1974), a definitive biography; Tyler Dennett, *John Hay: From Poetry to Politics* (New York: Dodd, Mead & Co., 1933); Phillip C. Jessup, *Elihu Root*, 2 vols. (New York: Dodd, Mead & Co., 1938); Hermann Hagedorn, *Leonard Wood*, 2 vols. (New York and London: Harper & Bros.,

1931); Jack C. Lane, *Armed Progressive: General Leonard Wood* (San Rafael, Calif., and London: Presidio Press, 1978).

Useful studies for the foreign-policy context within which McKinley functioned are David F. Healey's *US Expansionism: The Imperialistic Urge in the 1890s* (Madison: University of Wisconsin Press, 1970); Robert L. Beisner's *From the Old Diplomacy to the New, 1865–1900* (New York: Thomas Y. Crowell, 1975); and James A. Field, Jr., "American Imperialism: The Worst Chapter in Almost Any Book," *American Historical Review* 83 (1978): 644–668.

There are few general overviews of McKinley's record in foreign affairs. *Threshold to American Internationalism: Essays on the Foreign Policies of William McKinley*, ed. Paolo E. Coletta (New York: Exposition Press, 1970), contains accurate narratives on the coming of the war, McKinley's wartime leadership, and the peace negotiations. Cornelius W. Vahle, Jr.'s "Congress, the President, and Overseas Expansion, 1897–1901" (Ph.D. dissertation, Georgetown University, 1967) is an interesting treatment of key episodes.

The improvement in Anglo-American relations during the McKinley years has received detailed attention. The central study is Charles S. Campbell, Jr.'s *Anglo-American Understanding, 1898–1903* (Baltimore, Md.: Johns Hopkins Press, 1957). Other valuable accounts are Robert G. Neale, *Great Britain and United States Expansion: 1898–1900* (East Lansing: Michigan State University Press, 1966); Bradford Perkins, *Great Rapprochement: England and the United States, 1895–1914* (New York: Atheneum, 1968); Stuart Anderson, *Race and Rapprochement: Anglo-Saxonism and Anglo-American Relations, 1895–1904* (Rutherford, N.J.: Fairleigh Dickson University Press, 1981).

On Hawaiian annexation, the following are helpful: Julius W. Pratt's *Expansionists of 1898: The Acquisition of Hawaii and the Spanish Islands* (Baltimore, Md.: Johns Hopkins Press, 1936); William A. Russ, Jr.'s *The Hawaiian Republic, 1894–98 and Its Struggle to Win Annexation* (Selinsgrove, Pa.: Susquehanna University Press, 1961); Merze Tate's *The United States and the Hawaiian Kingdom: A Political History* (New Haven, Conn.: Yale University Press, 1965); Thomas J. Osborne's *"Empire Can Wait": American Opposition to Hawaiian Annexation, 1893–1898* (Kent, Ohio: Kent State University Press, 1981); William Michael Morgan's "The Anti-Japanese Origins of the Hawaiian Annexation Treaty of 1897," *Diplomatic History* 6 (1982): 23–44.

For general accounts of the war, Henry Cabot Lodge, *The War with Spain* (New York and London: Harper & Bros., 1899), is the contemporary narrative of a senatorial Republican. French Ensor Chadwick, *The Relations of the United States and Spain: Diplomacy* (New York: Charles Scribner's Sons, 1909) and *The Relations of the United States and Spain: The Spanish-American War,* 2 vols. (New York: Charles Scribner's Sons, 1911), are encyclopedic and thorough. Walter Millis, *The Martial Spirit: A Study of Our War with Spain* (Boston: Literary Guild, 1931), is colorful, journalistic, and unreliable. David F. Trask, *The War with Spain in 1898* (New York: Macmillan Publishing Co., 1981), is the readable, balanced, and well-documented one-volume study of the conflict that has long been needed.

Joseph A. Fry, "William McKinley and the Coming of the Spanish-American War: A Study of the Besmirching and Redemption of an Historical Image," *Diplomatic History* 3 (1979): 77–97, is a lucid, persuasive introduction to the literature on McKinley's prewar leadership. John Layser Offner, "President McKinley and the Origins of the Spanish-American War" (Ph.D. dissertation, Pennsylvania State University, 1957), provides a pioneering analysis in the primary sources of what McKinley did in 1897/98. Every student in this field owes Offner a debt of gratitude. Ernest R. May, in *Imperial Democracy: The Emergence of America as a Great Power* (New York: Harcourt, Brace & World, 1961), uses foreign archival sources with great skill but is much weaker on domestic politics. His own evidence refutes the negative judgment on McKinley that he advances. Walter LaFeber, *The New Empire: An Interpretation of American Expansion, 1860–1898* (Ithaca, N.Y.: Cornell University Press, 1963), sees McKinley as purposeful and strong, stresses economic causation, and should be used cautiously on specific factual points. Howard Wayne Morgan, *America's Road to Empire: The War with Spain and Overseas Expansion* (New York: John Wiley, 1965), depicts McKinley as an effective president whose leadership before and during the war does not match the stereotype of weakness.

John A. S. Grenville and George Berkeley Young, *Politics, Strategy, and American Diplomacy: Studies in Foreign Policy, 1873–1917* (New Haven, Conn.: Yale University Press, 1966), have a perceptive chapter on McKinley and the onset of the war. Paul S. Holbo's "Presidential Leadership in Foreign Affairs: William McKinley and the Turpie-Foraker Amendment," *American Historical Review* 72 (1967): 1321–1335, is an important essay. Charles S. Campbell's *The Transformation of American Foreign Relations,*

1865–1900 (New York: Harper & Row, 1976) is an uneasy blend of contradictory conclusions about the war and about McKinley. For Spain's position see, Orestes Ferrara, *The Last Spanish War: Revelations in "Diplomacy"* (New York: Paisley Press, 1937). Thomas Hart Baker, Jr.'s "Imperial Finale: Crisis, Decolonization, and War in Spain, 1890–1898" (Ph.D. dissertation, Princeton University, 1977) is most revealing about Spanish policy.

For more detailed aspects of the prewar period, the following articles and books are useful on the question of the "yellow press": George W. Auxier, "Middle Western Newspapers and the Spanish-American War, 1895–1898," *Mississippi Valley Historical Review* 26 (1940): 523–534; Joseph E. Wisan, *The Cuban Crisis as Reflected in the New York Press* (New York: Columbia University Press, 1934); and Harold J. Sylvester, "The Kansas Press and the Coming of the Spanish-American War," *Historian* 31 (1969): 251–267. The argument about economic causes for the war can be followed in Julius W. Pratt, "American Business and the Spanish-American War," *Hispanic American Historical Review* 14 (1934): 163–201; Nancy O'Connor, "The Spanish-American War: A Reevaluation of Its Causes," *Science and Society* 22 (1958): 129–143; "The Spanish-American War: Business Recovery and the China Market: Selected Documents and Commentary," *Studies on the Left* 1 (1960): 58–64; Lewis L. Gould, "The Reick Telegram and the Spanish-American War: A Reappraisal," *Diplomatic History* 3 (1979): 193–199.

The Cuban side of the approaching conflict is developed in George W. Auxier, "The Propaganda Activities of the Cuban *Junta* in Precipitating the Spanish-American War, 1895–1898," *Hispanic American Historical Review* 19 (1939): 286–305; and Philip S. Foner, *The Spanish-Cuban-American War and the Birth of American Imperialism, 1895–1902*, 2 vols. (New York and London: Monthly Review Press, 1972). Foner contends that the Cubans could have won the rebellion without American assistance. Hyman G. Rickover, in *How the Battleship Maine Was Destroyed* (Washington: Department of the Navy, 1976), argues persuasively that an internal explosion caused the ship to sink. Paul S. Holbo, "The Convergence of Moods and the Cuban-Bond 'Conspiracy' of 1898," *Journal of American History* 55 (1968): 54–72, adroitly recreates the atmosphere in which congressional deliberations over the coming of the war occurred.

On the war itself, Gerald F. Linderman's *The Mirror of War: American Society and the Spanish-American War* (Ann Arbor:

University of Michigan Press, 1974) is a group of interpretive essays. For McKinley's activities see Ida M. Tarbell, "President McKinley in War Times," *McClure's Magazine* 11 (1898): 209–224, and De B. Randolph Keim, "The President's War," *Frank Leslie's Popular Monthly* 50 (1900): 107–122. On the military aspects of the conflict, Graham A. Cosmas's *An Army for Empire: The United States Army in the Spanish-American War* (Columbia: University of Missouri Press, 1971) is the standard work. See also Edward Ranson's "The Investigation of the War Department, 1898–99," *Historian* 34 (1971): 78–99, and Edward F. Keuchel's "Chemicals and Meat: The Embalmed Beef Scandal of the Spanish-American War," *Bulletin of the History of Medicine* 48 (1974): 249–264. Willard B. Gatewood, Jr., comp., *"Smoked Yankees" and the Struggle for Empire: Letters from Negro Soldiers, 1898–1902* (Urbana: University of Illinois Press, 1971), is an informative collection of primary materials.

Contemporary accounts of the army's role include George Kennan's *Campaigning in Cuba* (New York: Century Co., 1899; reprint ed., Port Washington, N.Y.: Kennikat Press, 1971); John D. Miley, *In Cuba with Shafter* (New York: Charles Scribner's Sons, 1899); Charles Johnson Post, *The Little War of Private Post* (Boston: Little, Brown, 1960).

David F. Trask, *The War with Spain in 1898,* is excellent on the naval side. See also William R. Braisted, *The United States Navy in the Pacific, 1897–1909* (Austin: University of Texas Press, 1958), and Walter R. Herrick, Jr., *The American Naval Revolution* (Baton Rouge: Louisiana State University Press, 1966).

American postwar policy in Cuba is discussed by David F. Healy in *The United States in Cuba, 1898–1902: Generals, Politicians, and the Search for Policy* (Madison: University of Wisconsin Press, 1963) and by James H. Hitchman in *Leonard Wood and Cuban Independence, 1898–1902* (The Hague: Martinus Nijhoff, 1971).

The scholarship on the Philippines is growing rapidly. For the debate over the naval war plan to attack the islands, John A. S. Grenville, "American Naval Preparations for War with Spain, 1896–1898," *Journal of American Studies* 2 (1968): 33–47, and Ronald Spector, "Who Planned the Attack on Manila Bay?" *Mid-America* 53 (1971): 94–102, provide indispensable data. Phil Lyman Snyder's "Mission, Empire, or Force of Circumstances? A Study of the American Decision to Annex the Philippine Islands" (Ph.D. dissertation, Stanford University, 1971) is critical of McKinley but recognizes his key role. Older, but very much worth reading, are Paolo E. Coletta's two articles "Bryan, McKinley, and the Treaty of Paris," *Pacific Historical Review* 26 (1957): 131–146, and "McKinley, the Peace Negotiations, and the Acquisition of the Philippines," *Pacific Historical Review* 30 (1961): 341–350. On the Paris talks, *Making Peace with Spain: The Diary of Whitelaw Reid, September–December 1898*, ed. H. Wayne Morgan (Austin: University of Texas Press, 1965), is valuable. Brian Paul Damiani, in "Advocates of Empire: William McKinley, the Senate, and American Expansion, 1898–1899" (Ph.D. dissertation, University of Delaware, 1978), sees McKinley as cautious and tentative. Richard E. Welch, Jr.'s *George Frisbie Hoar and the Half-Breed Republicans* (Cambridge, Mass.: Harvard University Press, 1971) is important for the ratification struggle.

John Morgan Gates's *Schoolbooks and Krags: The United States Army in the Philippines, 1898–1902* (Westport, Conn.: Greenwood Press, 1973) is a balanced review of the military record. Richard E. Welch, Jr.'s *Response to Imperialism: The United States and the Philippine-American War, 1899–1902* (Chapel Hill: University of North Carolina Press, 1979) is a judicious, convincing account.

The debate over anti-imperialism has attracted many scholars. Robert L. Beisner's *Twelve against Empire: The Anti-Imperialists, 1898–1900* (New York: McGraw-Hill, 1968) is more graceful than it is penetrating. E. Berkeley Tompkins, *Anti-Imperialism in the United States: The Great Debate, 1890–1920* (Philadelphia: University of Pennsylvania Press, 1970), is thorough. Daniel B. Schirmer, *Republic or Empire: American Resistance to the Philippine War* (Cambridge, Mass.: Schenkman Publishing Co., 1972), is polemical. Relevant articles include: Fred H. Harrington, "The Anti-Imperialist Movement in the United States, 1898–1900," *Mississippi Valley Historical Review* 22 (1935): 211–230; Christopher Lasch, "The Anti-Imperialists, the Philippines, and the Inequality of Man," *Journal of Southern History* 24 (1958): 319–331; Robert L. Beisner, "1898 and 1968: The Anti-Imperialists and the Doves," *Political Science Quarterly* 85 (1970): 187–216.

On American governance of the Philippines under McKinley, the following are informative: Peter W. Stanley, *A Nation in the Making: The Philippines and the United States, 1899–1921* (Cambridge, Mass.: Harvard University Press, 1974); Virginia Frances Mulrooney, "No Victor, No Vanquished: United States Military Government in the Philippine Islands, 1898–1901" (Ph.D. dissertation, University of California at Los Angeles, 1975); Glenn Anthony May, *Social Engineering in the Philippines: The Aims, Execution, and Impact of American Colonial Policy, 1900–1913* (Westport, Conn.: Greenwood Press, 1980).

The most important studies of the administration's Far Eastern policy are Thomas J. McCormick's *China Market: America's Quest for Informal Empire, 1893–1901* (Chicago: Quadrangle Books, 1967), and Marilyn Blatt Young's *Rhetoric of Empire: American China Policy, 1895–1901* (Cambridge, Mass.: Harvard University Press, 1968). Peter W. Stanley's "The Making of an American Sinologist: William W. Rockhill and the Open Door," in *Perspectives in American History,* ed. Donald Fleming, vol. 11 (Cambridge, Mass.: Charles Warren Center for Studies in American History, 1978), pp. 419–460, is the most recent contribution to the literature on the Open Door.

Index